TELL ME HOW TO HEAR

God's Voice

You can receive detailed direction everyday

MARTY CARROLL

ALL *of* YOUR
HEART

Tell Me How to Hear God's Voice
Copyright © 2015 Marty Carroll

Published by:
All Of Your Heart
www.allofyourheart.org

Front cover design by Micah Carroll, Mykkah Photography, www.mykkah.com
Cover image: Abstract | www.shutterstock.com
Back cover; Interior design and production by Lisa Von De Linde, LisaVdesigns, www.lisavdesigns.com
Author photo: Mykkah Photography

This edition: ISBN 978-0-9909067-1-1 (softcover)

Library of Congress Control Number: 2015900353

Printed in the United States of America

Dedication

For my Mom, my pacesetter, Winnyfred Casement,

Following Jesus has never been difficult; I have followed you. From Proverbs 4:11-13: You have taught me the way of wisdom and led me along straight paths. Walking behind you, my steps have not been hampered. Running behind you, I have never stumbled. May your children's children cling to instruction and guard her as you have and in so doing, pave a glorious highway to Heaven. Keep running Mom; I'm right behind you and we're almost home!

And my children: For Christy, my constant cheerleader, for Charlie, my techy connection to the writer's world and for Micah, my colorful, cover creator. Thank you for everything you've done to get your Mom and this book across the finish line. You and yours are my great reward

TABLE OF CONTENTS

PREFACE

On the subject of books I have read two kinds. Sitting on my shelves are those that testify to the incredible gift of another human being. Through these books, various authors captured my interest and evoked my admiration. Then there are the other kind: Treasured volumes that testify of the incredible power of the living God. Through these, God captured my heart and evoked my worship. I pray this book will be that kind of book for you.

You may believe distance exists between God and yourself for a personal reason, a failure of some kind. Perhaps the pace of life has worn holes in your soul and left you with passive plodding: Your devotions are dry. The sermons you hear don't motivate you to live differently than the world. You're not sure exactly what's wrong. Your friends are no more excited about faith and God than you are. Maybe "dry and disciplined" is the way it is for everybody.

These possibilities represent the familiar merry-go-round of reasoning we use to explain away the reality that many of us are endeavoring to live "Christian lives" without intimacy and power. We get off a dizzying ride of personal questions and find ourselves full of frustration, wondering why our spiritual life isn't exciting and satisfying.

I know the frustration well. I spent bewildering years in the desert of dry faith because I believed knowledge about God would result in the power-filled life we hear about. It doesn't.

As the eldest of three preacher's daughters, I literally grew up in a church building. When we weren't in services, my sisters and I were rolling up and down the hallways in a secretary's chair. If not inside, we were outside the building roller-skating in the parking lot. Here, in our home away from home, my parents birthed one of the largest Christian schools in America today. Accordingly, I received a rich Christian education.

Since then, I have absorbed instruction from many of America's greatest Christian preachers and teachers. I have faithfully attended a local body of believers and been privileged to serve as a Sunday School teacher and public speaker for various age groups. The Body of Christ at large has been well watered. One thing is sure: If knowledge about God resulted in the power-filled life we hear about, I would have experienced it long ago. This dousing with Truth has not resulted in our falling deeply in love with Jesus. It has not impacted our ability to overcome personal sin, or compelled us to live for the glory of God.

Yet giving up is an elusive option. Just about the time we decide to cease our pursuit of intimacy and join the ranks of the complacent, that unsettled feeling returns; that unrelenting tug from somewhere deep inside that eerily whispers, *There's more.*

Regardless of what shape your faith is in, one wonderful aspect of being a genuine Christian is the reality that we carry Zoë life in our mortal flesh—the vitality of the life of God Himself. And Zoë life contains unlimited capacity to sprout *new life*—just like seed. Although we may not feel it, every seed of truth planted in our hearts retains the power-filled potential for growth and change.

Importantly, we should also acknowledge that life sprouts from seed because it's buried in dark earth. Endured any dark days lately? God hasn't forgotten you. Being buried may not be on your "bucket list" but I know from enduring my own dark season that those periods are a small price to pay for the *new life*—the *hope* that's burst from my heart. The analogy holds true: The Son has drawn me from darkness to light; God has drawn me to Himself. Yes, these days I'm soaking in the Son-shine and walking in a sense of freedom that only a power filled, intimate relationship with Jesus can provide. And I'm oh so happy to be free from the solitary confinement of the heart that dark circumstances can create.

Some of us are personally responsible for the dark places we find ourselves in today. Others of us are certain we never did anything to deserve the sentence. And if you've been there, you know your own heart can become a prison place of aloneness like no other.

Have you ever revisited a favorite place where happy memories were made (a former home, work place or vacation spot) only to find that now—because of some change—it has the opposite effect? Instead of making you feel secure, it magnifies your sense of aloneness. We avoid such places.

What do you do, then, when circumstances change the way you feel about the secure place of your own heart; the private chamber where the sweetest dreams and plans for the future are made? At one time or another, everyone's heart has been a favorite place. From here, we venture in and out with great hope of making all we chart in secret, a satisfying reality.

Then, one day, without warning we try the door and find it sealed. In one moment, some cruel circumstance turns our heart into a prison by denying us the freedom to walk out the dreams we've cherished. In the darkness, our dreams begin to disappear and so does our hope of ever being happy again. What do you do when the room of your own heart magnifies your sense of aloneness?

Perhaps you've picked up this book because you're in a prison you're desperate to escape. You're hoping it really is possible for regular people to hear clearly from God because you know it's going to take the detailed direction of His voice to lead you to real freedom. If that's the case, there is good news. God is anxious to speak clearly to you. He is anxious to direct you to the skylight of freedom that exists for every hurting heart. Ironically, anyone can escape through this skylight at anytime. All God asks is that we listen for His direction, look up in faith and obediently grab His strong hand.

I know, firsthand, that you can enjoy complete freedom and satisfaction today even if your circumstances do not change. Mine didn't. But I'm still excited about tomorrow; loving this life. I have made it up and through the skylight by allowing God's voice to direct the details of my day. And I'm full of hope because His voice is leading me back to His land of dreams for me. Consequently, I've never been more content. God wants you, as well, to experience the peace and contentment His Presence and purposes provide in these uncertain days.

Several pastor-teachers I greatly respect have written books about how to hear God's voice. Others have addressed it in their sermons. After listening, I believe there are many practical aspects of understanding that haven't been made clear. When the words "How To" are used, I always hope for very specific instruction. This book contains *very specific instruction.*

If you are not quite sure you really need to be able to hear God's voice, consider these situations: (1) What do you do about a discipline issue between children when you didn't witness the offense? (2) What opportunity do you take in a day when two equally appealing ones are offered? (3) What route do you take to a critical destination when you have more than one option? (4) What responsibility should be handled first when all of them have serious consequences?

What is the single greatest reason for learning to hear God's voice? It enables you to fall deeply in love with Jesus. And being in love with Him *fixes everything.*

Remember the early days of being in love? Nothing was insurmountable; term papers, even trips to the dentist didn't matter much. All of life seemed to sparkle with a special glow. Yep, that's my life. My ability to hear God's voice, coupled with a new understanding of the word "trust" has changed everything.

A quick note before you start: I use various translations of Scripture throughout this book, depending on the subject matter at hand.

Ready? Let's get started.

CHAPTER 1

Unstable In All Our Ways

I have always enjoyed watching people. Perhaps that's why Mom was careful to teach my sisters and me that it wasn't polite to stare. We grew up as preacher's daughters. And believe me—in a large congregation, there was plenty to stare at, from a little girl's height.

Specifically, the cheek pinchers were intriguing. You know them—those older folks who find children's round cheeks irresistible. Everything about them was interesting; their hats, their hankies, the big purses some carried and especially the large eyes that smiled through their glasses when they stooped to shout hello.

Now a cheek pincher myself, I especially love watching people in an airport or shopping mall. As they walk by, you can certainly learn a lot about popular fashion—or not.

Undoubtedly though, you learn the most by watching people's faces. At a glance, you know which ones are happy and which ones are not. You know which ones are married and which ones definitely are not. And, depending on whether or not you're in the mood to talk, you know which ones to sit by and which ones to run by.

How about you? Do you like watching people? And, if so, have you noticed anything different lately?

Recently I stood in a crowded checkout lane at a grocery store. And in those minutes, I noticed something very different about the people packed around me. These random faces that were normally distant and preoccupied were actually demonstrating a desire to be personal. Now you've got to admit, in this culture—that's different.

Not that there was a party mood. I still sensed tension; that underlying uneasiness we all seem to be living with while we wait to find out what's coming next for our country. Our questions about the future have etched noticeable anxiety on faces and laced our casual conversations with fear. Clearly, no one knows what to expect.

The catastrophic changes in our economy are creating stress everywhere. Lines are long and fuses are short. Health magazines, tell us stress-related illnesses are on the rise, in spite of all the exercise we're doing to avoid them. And that's no surprise. Physical illness is a natural consequence of living with prolonged conflict. To one degree or another, we are all living with the conflict of trying to prepare for a future that's completely uncertain.

The positive outcome, though, is what I noticed in the check out line: our uncertainty over what's coming next is coaxing us to reach out to each other. People want to know if everybody else is feeling the way they are. They want to talk about what's bothering them; hoping someone has a suggestion or piece of information that will relieve their anxiety. And they're desperate enough to strike up conversations with total strangers to find out.

Perhaps, "we the people" are finally remembering the value of the brotherhood of man—of having and being a brother and a neighbor.

A Divine Explanation

In the midst of the present chaos and stress, there is good news: The pain of *any* conflict can be resolved once you identify its source. And, in Haggai 2:6-7 (NKJV), God identifies the source of the instability we sense:

For thus says the LORD of hosts: "Once more... I will shake heaven and earth, the sea and dry land; and I will shake all nations, and they shall come to the Desire of All Nations..."

The recent pounding of natural disasters makes it hard to deny that God is shaking the nations. Gratefully for us, the Bible makes it clear that one day a hopeful end will come to the devastation we are witnessing. Yet, just as clear is the reality that, before things get eternally better, they are temporarily going to get a whole lot worse. As I often say, every time we pray the words, "Thy kingdom come," we ask God to advance the holocaust of events that will bring life on Earth, as we know it, to an end.

Speaking of end-time events, I teach the elementary-age children at the church where my eldest son pastors. Recently, I spent seven weeks teaching them eschatology—the big word for end-time events. They loved it. High voices and jumping feet had them bouncing off the walls when we talked about the trumpet blast that starts it all. They can't wait to be caught away to meet Jesus in the air. What child wouldn't be excited about getting to fly?

Clearly, all of us should be listening for the sound of a trumpet. But until we hear it, the painful birth pangs leading up to Jesus' return are going to be reality for us.

Because that's true, may I ask you another question? How are you personally dealing with the daily pressure, stress and fear that this unstable time in history is creating for you? Although hiding under a pillow sounds good, it doesn't make it easier to sleep at night.

There are endless questions and few answers. Should we invest in gold, silver and stock, or save our cash? What do we do about needs as basic as food and housing? Is there any way to safeguard the job we have or will anything we do matter? As a result of all we are hearing, are there steps we should be taking to secure future needs for education and retirement? Or are there any safe steps left to take?

Tragically, history has been repeated in America. And it's safe to say, everyone is struggling to be hopeful about tomorrow. We have seen, clearly, that the best-laid financial plans are no guarantee for anyone's future. A familiar verse in I Corinthians 15:19 (KJV) says it all:

> *If in this life only we have hope...we are of all men most miserable.*

It's understandable that people hold America's problems responsible for the foreboding sense of uncertainty I just described. They believe problems like that of our crippled economy and the threat of nuclear war have created our nation's instability.

Yet, America's stability has never rested on the wealth of its economy or strength of its homeland security. Whether her citizens have acknowledged it or not, *America's stability has always rested on her reverence for God and the ordinances of His Holy Word.*

The voice of our country's rich history testifies to the stability of a nation "whose God is the Lord". As a God-fearing nation, America was held fast through the economic collapse of the Great Depression and from the enemies of two world wars.

However, America no longer fears God. As a nation, we neither revere Him nor regard His plan. The only plans citizens, at large, regard today are their own. And that reality puts our nation in serious jeopardy because nations and people were never made for their own plans. The nations of the world and those of us in them were specifically designed for the righteous plans of God. Scripturally stated:

> *The Lord hath made all things for himself.*
> PROVERBS 16:4 (KJV)

That truth alone explains the ominous sense of instability and isolation we sense everywhere we go. Tangible tension prevails because America continues to choose to live in open rebellion to the revealed plan of God, contained in the Bible. It is not our imagination. Our nation's foundation *is* shaking.

One decision at a time, our stability is being successfully, and systematically destroyed, as "We the People" continue to exchange our trust in God for trust in ourselves; choosing to do what seems right in our own eyes.

They traded the truth about God for a lie. So they worshiped and served the things God created instead of the Creator himself.
ROMANS 1:25

And Psalm 11:3 (KJV) goes on to say:

If the foundations be destroyed, what can the righteous do?

We had better do something. For, with each new piece of legislation that passes to intentionally separate us from the truth that has held us fast, we invite God—by His absence—to shake our nation with disaster.

The stability we long for that withstands the wind of adversity only comes from being anchored to trust in God. That is why solving America's problems will not restore America's stability. For her stability to be restored, America must return her trust to God.

The Ability to Maintain Stability

The wrath of God toward sin is shaking the nations in an attempt to wake people up. Sadly, it appears to be the only way nations will rouse to truth, repent and call on His name.

Making it personal, regardless of what happens to our nation at large, each of us can attain and maintain personal stability for ourselves. Hell itself cannot shake the soul of the Christian that chooses to entrust all they are and have to the refuge of God's plans.

Reverence for God gives a man deep strength; his children have a place of refuge and security.

PROVERBS 14:26

In the refuge of God's personal plans, anyone can experience the peace and stability that defies human understanding. And, mercifully for us all, the steady hand of God remains extended to guide us there.

For all this, his anger is not turned away, but his hand is **stretched out still***.*

ISAIAH 5:25 (KJV), emphasis added

God alone is the only refuge in times of trouble because *all power belongs to Him.* And because it does, no power can prevail against His plans, or destroy those of us who are abiding in them. From Psalm 33 we read:

...with a breath He can scatter the plans of all the nations who oppose Him, but His own plan stands forever. His intentions are the same for every generation... great strength is not enough to save anyone...But the eyes of the Lord are watching over those who fear Him, who rely upon His steady love. He will keep them from death even in times of famine...Only He can help us...Yes Lord, let your constant love surround us, for our hopes are in you alone.

It has been said, "Security is not the absence of danger but the Presence of God no matter what the danger."[1] Because time is running out and eternity will soon begin, there has never been a time in the history of the world when the power and stability, of God's specific direction, has been more critical for us to possess.

Whose plans are you committed to? It's an important question. It's an important question because the answer determines whether or not you have current and future access to the only fallout shelter that exists.

Hide your loved ones in the shelter of your Presence, safe beneath your hand, safe from all conspiring men. Blessed is the Lord, for he has shown me that his never-failing love protects me like the walls of a fort!

PSALM 31:20

If you are going to experience the security and stability of God's protective power in your daily life, you must know how to identify God's plans, large and small and be committed to them. And anyone can identify those plans and take refuge in them when they know how to *identify His voice*.

Each day, as I make the effort to identify and obey God's voice, I am swept into the force field of power that surrounds His plan for me. And it's the reality of His Presence and power, in these daily places, that continues to give me the strength I need to face the instability and uncertainties of the future with courage and hope.

Recently, I heard a well-known Pastor, whom I respect say, "It would be nice if we all had a direct, daily revelation of what God wants us to do."

Immediately, I got concerned. *Uh oh, I do receive daily revelations of what God wants me to do. Is he suggesting that's bad—or is one of us missing something?*

Not only is it "nice" to receive daily revelations of what God wants us to do—I know it to be absolutely necessary; necessary for receiving the stabilizing power we've been talking about. And further, it's necessary for accomplishing the specific work of God's Kingdom for which each of us was uniquely created!

I do receive daily, detailed, direct revelation from the voice of God's Holy Spirit. And you know what? It is just as wonderful as it sounds!

I have written this book because I believe it's God's will that we all receive direct, daily revelation from God regarding the details of our day.

America was born because courageous men and women knew how to be precisely guided by God. And I believe our Nation has ground to a spiritually powerless halt today because we have lost the ability to discern the guidance of His voice.

Again, if we are going to fix any problem, we have to start by identifying where we've gone wrong. To restore our personal and national stability, we must choose to get in step with the power that surrounds God's plan. To identify God's daily plans, we must know how to identify the direction of God's Spirit—His Voice!

CHAPTER 2

Where Have All the Soldiers Gone?

Recently, I walked through the family room and noticed I'd left the television on. As I backed up to turn it off, I became entranced in the closing minutes of an old black and white movie that featured Greer Garson.

The story portrayed a British family's struggle to survive the death and devastation of WWII. This final scene pictured them in the bombed ruins of their small church. There, courageously clutching hymnals, they stood together singing with other grieving families.

As they sang, the camera panned away to a gaping hole in the roof where hanging rafters framed a closing picture of hope. The splintered skylight revealed allied planes roaring above them in a V-formation. And over the drone of the engines, the families triumphantly sang "Onward Christian Soldiers".

I smiled. As the credits rolled, countless pictures came to mind. I daydreamed about boisterously singing that song, myself, when I was a little girl marching around pews with my Sunday school class.

At some point in my daydreaming, though, I stopped smiling. My happy memories faded into somber thoughts of how America has changed in my lifetime. How hard it has become, to find those

"Christian Soldiers" we used to sing about—you know, the people with a warrior's heart; people willing to fight and suffer if necessary, for the sake of what's important to God.

How many do you know? How many Christian warriors would you say there are in your circle of friends? Would you dare consider yourself one?

Paul was certainly the Christian warrior of his day. While writing the letter that became II Timothy, he encouraged a fellow warrior in his circle of friends.

We get a clear picture of what a warrior's heart looks like when Paul declares in II Timothy 2:10 (AMP):

> *Therefore **I am ready** to persevere and stand my ground with patience and **endure everything** for the sake of God's chosen, so that they too may obtain the salvation which is in Christ Jesus, with the reward of eternal glory.*
>
> emphasis added

Ready or not, the fulfillment of Biblical prophecy that currently headlines our evening news indicates life is about to change drastically. Few Christians would argue that we are living in the last days of the Church Age—the time between Jesus' return to Heaven and Christians being caught away to meet Jesus in the air. God is rapidly drawing this age to a close. And, as His kingdom advances, undeniable darkness is increasing as the final battles are waged for the souls of men.

What does that mean for you and me? Exactly what does God expect us to do, in light of this escalating war between the Prince of Darkness and the Son of God? God has every intention that we pick up the glistening Sword of His Spirit and get in the thick of things. And, yes—get in it—to win it. We are here to carry the light of the life of God to those who remain lost in darkness, so, as Paul said, "they too can find the Savior."

And because this is our purpose, every true Christian whose heart beats beside God's Spirit in them should anticipate the enemy's defiance.

We are troubled on every side, yet not distressed; we are perplexed, but not in despair.

II CORINTHIANS 4:8 (KJV)

Satan is not confused about *his* purpose. He has a clear understanding of the great damage one God-possessed life can do to his kingdom. He has watched Christian soldiers successfully penetrate enemy lines at night. He has shielded his eyes as their explosions of light obliterated his carefully constructed strongholds of darkness. And for these rage-provoking reasons, he takes any opportunity to level his demonic crosshairs on the heart of every passionate Christian soldier.

If we don't want to end up cowering on the backside of a hill, like David's brothers did when Goliath taunted them, we had better do our homework and know our enemy. More importantly, we had better know how to access the only power that defeats that enemy.

How does Satan take down the best of the best? His arsenal of deception is vast, but he has one particular plan that's tried and true. It requires little effort on his part and is extremely effective in taking out Christian soldiers.

As the ultimate strategist, Satan certainly knows better than to announce his presence among our ranks. Why give a soldier the opportunity to defend himself? He much prefers waiting in diabolical delight for the unsuspecting opportunity that boredom in the barracks provides. Accordingly, he takes his place in the mundane activities of regular days where all soldiers must spend time.

Then, when discontent is high and spirits are low, he discretely offers a casual suggestion to the passionate Christian soldier. "Why not get some air? Why not take a few minutes to breathe in the satisfying pleasures of this world to pass the time—just until orders arrive? You deserve a break."

To many a frustrated soldier, the suggestion sounds harmless enough. What could it possibly hurt? Why not?

Thus armed with momentary confidence in his own strength, our would-be warrior consents to briefly step outside. Stretching his restless arms into the air, he takes in one deep breath and then another. And as he does, the odorless fumes of sin's intoxicating pleasure fill his lungs. Far sooner than he could have imagined, the addictive fumes displace the vital breath of his holy passion until the enemy's work is finished. Playing follow the leader, one soldier after another now follows suit.

Soon, Satan himself is able to step out of the shadows into plain view. And when he does, oddly, no soldier runs for a weapon. The would-be warriors, who once posed such a threat, are now safely drugged with indifference to the Commander of Heaven's desires. Disoriented by a fog of spiritual stupor, Satan leads them off into darkness, where the master of sin requires they serve as slaves to their own desires.

Look around. You can see for yourself that Satan's plan is enjoying great success. American Christians, in general, are not hungry for God. They are hungry for money and entertainment.

> "...Come on, let's have some fun! Let's go hear him tell us what the Lord is saying!" So they come as though they are sincere and sit before you listening. But they have no intention of doing what I tell them to; they talk very sweetly about loving the Lord, but with their hearts they are loving their money.
> EZEKIEL 33:30-31

And the particular entertainment they're paying for indicates they are just as interested in sensual satisfaction as non-Christians. Christians are shying away from courageous steps of faith to take only the baby steps they believe are necessary to gain entrance into heaven.

The Reason for Powerless Faith

Where do we go from here? Only God knows what it will take to restore our passion for living righteously before Him. Jesus said:

And because iniquity shall abound, the love of many shall wax cold.

MATTHEW 24:12 (KJV)

The chilling wind of the world's influence is so great the light of God's power, in our churches, is dim. And, because the church appears to be powerless, chairs are empty. Hurting people are not running for the gospel. Instead, they run blindly for what the world offers.

…whose minds the god of this age has blinded, who do not believe, lest the light of the gospel of Christ, who is the image of God should shine on them.

II CORINTHIANS 4:4 (NKJV)

We must wake up from our stupor of indifference.

*Those in frequent contact with the exciting things the world offers should make good use of their opportunities **without stopping to enjoy them**; for the world in its present form will soon be gone.*

I CORINTHIANS 7:31, emphasis added

There is a simple explanation for the spiritual darkness that blankets the Earth and even the church. Sadly, it exists because the light of God, in individual hearts, is dim.

*"…If then the light that is in **you** is darkness, how **great** is that darkness!"*

MATTHEW 6:23 (NKJV), emphasis added

Why is the light of God dim in individual hearts? I believe personal faith has become powerless faith because Christians see Jesus as a subject to be studied, rather than a person to be known.

Initially, it surprised me to learn from an ABC news poll[2] that 83% of Americans consider themselves to be Christians—followers of Jesus Christ. Yet, as I thought more about it, I concluded it wasn't that surprising after all.

In churches across America, people are allowed to believe they have a relationship with God if at some point they repeated the words of a sinner's prayer, read parts of the Bible, and attended church on occasion. Although these activities are vital components of a relationship with God, they certainly don't constitute one.

Consider how far that format would take you in establishing a meaningful relationship with another human being. How well could you get to know someone if your efforts consisted of making a declaration to them, reading parts of their autobiography, and listening to other people talk about them? You could call it whatever you wanted, but it certainly would not be accurate to call it a "relationship".

And in this fast-paced, lonely world, people aren't interested in empty relationships. They are desperate for meaningful ones. People want relationships that satisfy their deep desire to be loved and understood. No one's interested in chatter that's personally irrelevant. Had anyone walk away lately while you were in mid-sentence?

A true relationship is an alliance of commitment where the needs of two people are met. And, very simply, the success and strength of all meaningful love relationships pivots on two people's ability to communicate with one another.

Do you agree?

Don't forget that as you continue reading.

If you agree that communication is vital to human love relationships, how can you expect to fall in love with God without it? Where did we get the idea that communication with God was different? Some say they communicate with God because they engage in the one-way conversation of prayer when it's time for a meal, sleep, or personal devotions.

God, in the picture and person of Jesus, is not a subject to be studied. He is a *person* whose heart—just like the ones He has fashioned inside us—longs to be known.

My walk of faith convinces me that Christians must know how to identify *God's voice* to experience the deep satisfaction a love relationship with Him affords.

Short of a devastating nationwide disaster, I believe this intimate exchange of conversation with God alone, will course correct the powerless path Christians are following. At this late date, only *genuine intimacy* with God will cause Christians to lay down the hectic pursuit of the "good life" and pick up the purpose-filled pursuit of a Godly life.

Throw Me a Wrench

Several years ago, in the middle of a busy day, my youngest son yelled for me to come out to the garage. The urgency in his voice made me run to see what was up. I swung open the door to the garage and saw that his engine was what was "up"—in the air— swinging above him. My son stood where the engine used to be.

He had broken the entire car down to quart size bags of nuts and bolts, painted it blue, and was in the middle of the tedious process of putting it all back together again. At that moment, he needed his Mom to throw him a few tools and help guide the engine back into place. I enjoyed the truly personal nature of those greasy moments with my son.

The goal of this chapter is to inspire you to consider the personal nature of your relationship with God. The pace of life today is so intense, few Christians ever stop to consider how "personal" the nature of their relationship with God actually is—especially when their lives are running smoothly under their own control. This is probably true because few Christians have seen a genuinely intimate relationship with God modeled for them. They have few role models.

Thankfully, life has its own way of throwing a wrench in the engine of our independence from God. In particular, I have observed two obstacles that force us to cry out for God's help; that cause us to abruptly stop and consider how personal the nature of our relationship with God is.

What's the first one? It's the final, usually sudden, realization that we can't make ourselves happy. When you and I exhaust the warehouse of our own abilities and resources and find that only *personal unhappiness* remains, we are forced to consider the nature of our relationship with God. The story of the Prodigal Son paints a picture of this moment of truth.

The second obstacle that abruptly causes us to consider God's truth is *a crisis*; a disaster on the Earth, in our marriage or in our body. When crisis knocks at our door, we waste little time acknowledging we need God's personal help to fix things.

For he does not delight himself in the Almighty or pay any attention to God except in times of crisis.

JOB 27:10

When we come up against either of these obstacles, we find out in a hurry whether we have a personal relationship with Jesus or simply knowledge of Him. Rationalize it as we may, we have one or the other.

How sad, that it often takes an unhappy heart or a deeply wounded heart to ask the important questions of life. Questions like, "If my life is not going to guarantee me more happiness than this, what am I here for?"

Fortunately for us, when we're finally ready to ask the right question, God is more than ready to give us the right answer. His answer to that particular question is found in II Corinthians 4:10 (NKJV).

...that the life of Jesus also may be manifested in our body.

I responded to the Holy Spirit's Presence and trusted in Jesus to be my Savior when I was 5 years old. However, another 18 years passed before I asked the right question. I clearly remember the day I did.

Exhausted from trying, I finally admitted truth to God and myself: In spite of all my best efforts, I had failed at making myself happy. And, to my panic, I was not going to be able to outrun the tidal wave of destruction headed for the sand castle of my dreams; the castle of dreams I had built on my own. In the desperate moments of those days, my understanding became clear: I knew *a lot* about God but I did not know Him as a Person.

How about you? How *personal* is your relationship with God? It can be an uncomfortable question. Regardless of your answer, your heart's cry for intimacy with Him is all He's waiting for. When I became desperate for a truly *personal* relationship with God, He began to communicate directly with me. He taught me how to hear His voice. He will do the same for you.

> "...*you will find him, if you search after Him with **all** your heart and with **all** your soul.*"
>
> DEUTERONOMY 4:29 (ESV), emphasis added

In case you have questions about how God is able to communicate directly with people on Earth, let's stop to clarify. Second Chronicles 6 petitions God in three separate verses with these words:

> "*Hear from heaven where you live...*"

God the Father resides in Heaven. He sits on the throne of the Majesty on High, in a true tabernacle that exists there.

> ...*Christ, whose priesthood we have just described, is our High Priest, and is in heaven at the place of greatest honor next to God himself. He ministers in the **temple of heaven**,*

the true place of worship built by the Lord not by human hands.

HEBREWS 8:1-2, emphasis added

Where is Jesus? Jesus is in Heaven. This same passage of Scripture makes it clear that God's Son also dwells in that Tabernacle. Jesus is seated at His Father's right hand. From that *place*, He intercedes for us; He pleads with God on our behalf.

For He must remain in heaven until the final recovery of all things from sin, as prophesied from ancient times.

ACTS 3:21

It is God's Spirit who is everywhere at the same time. He is the third person of the Trinity. It is *God, The Holy Spirit,* who communicates with us. Jesus made it clear to His disciples, in John 16:7 (NKJV), that He was returning to Heaven so that the Holy Spirit could descend to Earth to be with us.

"Nevertheless I tell you the truth. It is to your advantage that I go away; for if I do not go away, the Helper will not come to you; but if I depart, I will send Him to you."

It is God's own Spirit, again *The Holy Spirit* that tells us what God thinks. The Holy Spirit tells us what God's desire or will is for us.

*No one can know God's own thoughts except God's own Spirit. And God has actually **given us** His Spirit to **tell us** about the wonderful free gifts of grace and blessing that God has given us.*

I CORINTHIANS 2:11, emphasis added

In addition to telling us God's desires, the Holy Spirit teaches us the truths of God:

...the Holy Spirit...lives within you, so you don't need anyone to teach you what is true. For the Spirit teaches you everything you need to know, and what He teaches is true— it is not a lie.

I JOHN 2:27

Again, by God's grace, when I became desperate for a *relationship* with God—finally and *fully surrendering* my life to Him—His Spirit began teaching me how to identify when God was speaking to me.

In my first lesson, God simply asked me to acknowledge that every action I took was preceded by a thought I was able to hear. Secondly, He taught me that all the thoughts I heard—directing me to take some action—were coming from one of two sources. Finally, He taught me how to capture a thought and identify whether or not it was coming from Him. II Corinthians 10:5 (ESV) indicates that it is possible to capture thoughts:

We destroy arguments and every lofty opinion raised against the knowledge of God, and take every thought captive to obey Christ,

This verse challenges us to capture thoughts and then consider the thoughts we capture; making sure they reflect submission to Jesus.

Wonderfully, when we identify that a particular thought of direction is coming from God's Spirit and 'walk-it-out', we walk in the Spirit as instructed in Galatians 5:16. Walking in the Spirit has many benefits. Greatest of all:

*...those who follow after the Holy Spirit find themselves **doing those things** that please God....For all who are led by the Spirit of God are the sons of God.*

ROMANS 8:5 & 14, emphasis added

God would not admonish us to be led by His Spirit if it wasn't possible for us to receive direction *from* His Spirit. And, very simply, we receive His direction through the same exchange of written and verbal communication that comprises all relationships. After all, we were made first and foremost for a relationship of fellowship with God.

Jesus is not a subject to be studied. He is a person to be known. How do we fix the problem of powerless faith in individual hearts? Powerless faith can be converted to powerful faith in the split second it takes to choose *radical obedience to God.* Tall order? Not really. Radical obedience is the natural result of passionate love. To love God passionately, He must be real to you. *Hearing God's voice reveals His reality.*

I witness the power of God in my daily activity because I am walking out a life of radical obedience. I walk in radical obedience because I now love God passionately. I have fallen passionately in love with God because He is real to me. He is real to me because I know how to hear His voice!

"My sheep hear my voice…"

JOHN 10:27 (NKJV)

CHAPTER 3

The Sufficiency of Scripture

Doesn't the Bible provide daily direction for us? Why do we need to identify the Holy Spirit's voice? II Timothy 3:16 (NASB) says:

All Scripture is inspired by God and profitable for teaching, for reproof, for correction, for training in righteousness.

Scripture is wholly sufficient for training us to live righteous lives that please God. My faith rests on the solid doctrines of God's written Word. It is every Christian's responsibility to know the doctrines of Scripture.

Further, God's Word is the central tenet of divine revelation. In other words, it is the supreme authority in revealing who God is to us. And, as our supreme authority, Scripture teaches that our ability to gain the knowledge of God is assisted by the work of the Holy Spirit.

I Corinthians 2 (NKJV) attests to this truth. Consider verses 10, 11 & 12:

*But God has revealed **them** to us through His Spirit. For the Spirit searches all things, yes, the deep things of God. For* *what man knows the things of a man except the spirit of the man which is in him? Even so no one knows the things of God except the Spirit of God. Now we have received, not the spirit of the world, but the Spirit who is from God, that we might know the things that have been freely given to us by God.*

Whether you believe this passage is describing the revelation of truth by the Holy Spirit to only the authors of Scripture or believe it is describing the revelation of truth by the Holy Spirit to every believer, these verses undeniably attribute the process of communication between God and man to the Holy Spirit.

Some theologians teach that God no longer speaks to us today apart from the Bible. They believe any teaching that suggests He *does* still speak, implies Scripture is not sufficient for training us to live righteous lives. They believe such teaching implies something else needs to be added to the Christian walk of faith. Certainly we are not to add to the inspired Word of God. Proverbs 30:6 (NKJV), says:

Do not add to His words, lest He rebuke you, and you be found a liar.

Yet, neither are we to subtract from it. And the trustworthy record of Scripture does contain teaching on God's desire to be known by the assisted work of the Holy Spirit.

When the Biblical Canon (the set of books chosen to be authoritative as Scripture) was comprised, one of the main criteria for the books selected was that the author of each book, be an eyewitness to the accounts they recorded. Most of the writers of the New Testament knew the Lord Jesus Christ personally. They were witnesses to the very words of God through His Son. These criteria authenticated God's words. That is an important reason why we call the Bible the inspired Word of God. The books in the Bible contain the very words of God, sealed in testimony by witnesses.

The record of Scripture is living and powerful. God divinely inspired the transcription of the Bible to preserve the pure truth and accuracy of His teaching; He gave us His Word to make His ordinances and laws clear. And He intends that we know what His Word says. But having knowledge of what the Bible says is not the intended end, in itself. Demons know what the Bible says.

The Bible exists to *reveal God* to us. God didn't give us the Bible so that His *words* could be known. He gave us the Bible so that *He* could be known.

Jesus said, in John 5:39 (AMP):

"You search and investigate and pore over the Scriptures diligently, because you suppose and trust that you have eternal life through them. And these [very Scriptures] testify about me!"

Paul said, in Philippians 3:8 (AMP):

*...I count everything as loss compared to the possession of the priceless privilege...of **knowing Christ Jesus my Lord** and of progressively becoming more deeply and intimately acquainted with Him...*

emphasis added

In no way do I seek to add to the inspired Word of God. This book is written to be a testimony and a tool in helping you discover that God does still speak today—through His written Word and by His Holy Spirit.

The Holy Scriptures contain the entirety of God's revelation to man about Himself and the Scriptures are infallible and inerrant. God does not speak today to impart new revelation about Himself. Rather, God speaks to illumine what has been revealed in Scripture and speaks to reveal direction for His will in our daily living here; God speaks to give every Christian personal, practical, specific direction for daily life. His Spirit gives the revelation and guidance necessary to align our lives with Scripture. And, as always, Scripture has the final authority.

If, for the cause of dispensational truth, you choose to believe God no longer speaks to any human being today for any reason apart from the written record of Scripture, the practical questions posed in chapter 7 will create some serious contemplation for you. Until then, because all Scripture is profitable for teaching and training in righteousness consider this verse:

> *See that you do not refuse Him who speaks. For if they did not escape, who refused Him who spoke on earth, much more shall we not escape, if we turn away from Him who speaks from Heaven,*
>
> HEBREWS 12:25 (NKJV)

How can this testimony of God's detailed direction by His voice, be proved? The existence and authenticity of God's specific direction, by the voice of His Holy Spirit, can be validated by the *God-honoring fruit it produces.*

God has not stopped communicating directly with His people. When Jesus paid the debt for our sins with His blood, the veil that separated us from God, the Father, was torn in two—giving us direct access to Him. II Corinthians 2:11 confirms that not only do we now have direct access to God's Presence, we have that access by way of containing His very own Spirit. And the Bible says His Spirit has a voice!

> *And the Holy Spirit, forever truthful, says it too. So we have these three witnesses; the voice of the Holy Spirit in our hearts, the voice from heaven at Christ's baptism, and the voice before he died. And they all say the same thing: that Jesus Christ is the Son of God.*
>
> I JOHN 5:6-8

This verse explains that the voice of the Holy Spirit in our heart is a witness to the truth that Jesus is God's Son. How could we not expect to have an exchange of conversation with God now that the voice and Presence of His own Spirit has taken up residence *in* us? God still speaks today for the same reason we speak to others we love. Love longs for intimate interchange.

I enjoy picking out new lovers in a restaurant. It's not hard. They're the ones talking instead of eating. No love deepens without communication. If human love is dependent on intimate interchange, how could it be that the heart of God—who Himself *is love*—could be satisfied by a few brief moments of formal one-way conversation during a week? We were created to keep company with the living God.

> *Blessed are the people who know the joyful sound! They walk,*
> *O Lord, in the light of your countenance.*
>
> PSALM 89:15 (NKJV)

Our faith must rest on God's inspired, written Word. And as it does, we must remember that God has given us His written Word in order that we might become intimately acquainted with Him. And intimate relationships are born from conversation between two hearts.

Do you have intimate two-way conversations with God?

It's an important question.

It's important because it's easy to confuse reverence for God with love for God. They are not the same. A person can possess deep reverence for God because of all they know about Him, yet fail to possess a passionate love for Him. I know it's possible because it was true of me.

After eighteen years of exposure to sound Biblical teaching, God was still not real to me. And may I say also by experience, that until God is *real* to you, *nothing the Bible has to say will matter enough to impact the decisions of your life.*

God *is* real to me, today. And I attribute that reality to the relationship of intimate conversation He has initiated with me. One night, years ago, as I reached to turn out the light beside my bed, the Holy Spirit spoke as clearly as I have ever heard Him speak. He said, *I am God, and I want to be known by you.*

In the dark stillness of that moment, I tried to take in the wonder of what I had just *heard.* I replayed the words over and over again. Could it really be that God was literally seeking love from me? My next emotion was one of overwhelming sadness. How could it be that the God of Heaven would have to *ask* to be known and loved?

How quickly we can forget that all of our desires—like the deep desire to be loved—are a reflection of our Creator's desires. God fashioned us, His children, after His own likeness, inwardly and outwardly. When was the last time you longed to feel loved and understood? God's heart longs for the understanding and love our passionate obedience alone can provide Him. We only demonstrate that we understand what's important to Him, when we do what He asks. Samuel spoke to Saul about God's need for our obedience when he said:

> *"Obedience is far better than sacrifice. He is much more interested in your listening to him than in your offering…"*
>
> I SAMUEL 15:22

Later that same week, as I read the Bible, I heard the same voice I'd heard in the darkness speak again. This time the Holy Spirit asked me to turn to several specific chapters in the book of Hosea. Curious as to why I was being directed to read *that* Old Testament passage, I quickly turned to it. Tears streamed down my face as God's inspired Word confirmed the spoken words I had heard several nights before.

"I don't want your sacrifices—I want your love; I don't want your offerings—I want you to know me."

HOSEA 6:6

God wants to be known by you. As you learn to identify His voice, and communicate with Him, passionate love will compel you to fulfill His personal desires; the mandates of His all-sufficient, written Word and those expressed by His own Holy Spirit.

CHAPTER 4

X Marks the Spot—Locating the Place of God's Power

In recent years, the word "change" has been used a lot in America's political discourse. Undoubtedly, that's because the word attracts instant attention, particularly in hard times. Like helium balloons, hearts fill with hope every time they hear it. And hope does float. Hearts are hungry for change because hearts are hungry for hope.

How we hope to escape pain. It's certainly not wrong to want God's power to free us from our painful circumstances. But it's a wake-up call for Christians when the strong desire for positive change makes *locating God's power the goal above loving His heart.* Sadly, many Christians have desired the one above the other. At one time I certainly did. My pain made me hungry for God's power—not necessarily His companionship.

Many well-meaning saints have the cart before the horse. But rest assured: You and I will never locate God's power and the relief from pain it represents until we have committed first to seeking

His heart. The keys to His Kingdom hang there. If we *could* access His power to drive the engine of our own plans, God knows His plans would never be accomplished on this sin-sick Earth. To hunt for the treasure of God's power in the dark soil of our own plans is more than a waste of time.

Yet, when we get first things first (in merciful irony) we'll discover that the very pain we sought power to escape is, in fact, the God-ordained map to the treasure we've desired all along. Be encouraged, committed Christian. When the circumstances of life suddenly change or refuse to change—leaving you uncomfortable or even hopeless—all is not lost. God is at work charting a map for your good.

As our Great Redeemer, Jesus eagerly waits to turn every hurtful experience on this sin-cursed Earth into a treasure we will one day be grateful for. In the same way scar tissue is stronger than tissue that hasn't been wounded, the scars of our life-wounds can leave us spiritually and emotionally stronger than we were before.

Growing up in church, I heard a lot of testimonies. For the most part, they all linked a grateful heart to painful scars. It never made sense to me. Who in their right mind was honestly grateful for pain? Come on!

Actually, it scared me.

And that made me mad.

To the point that, even after I entered dark tunnels of pain myself, I vowed I would never say what they had said.

But for years now I have been saying it: I *too* am grateful for the pain that has driven me to the power-filled treasure of a love relationship with Jesus. And, if I could, I sincerely would not exchange my circumstances for the sweetest plans I once had for myself.

How could I? I never once saw any sustaining, supernatural event explode in the middle of *my own* plans.

The Lord himself is my inheritance, my prize. He is my food and drink, my highest joy! ...he gives me wisdom in the night.

*He tells me what to do...You have let me experience the joys of
life and the exquisite pleasures of your own eternal presence.*

PSALM 16:5, 7 & 11

Regarding plans, I have written about the instability of our
nation and the anxiety it has created in people as they try to
establish their own. Further, I have shared that the stability and
peace of mind we need, to enjoy our lives, only comes as we
place the full weight of our trust in God.

Again, regardless of the choice America makes, you and I can
experience the stabilizing power of God in our own futures.

*The **steps** of a good man are ordered by the LORD...
Though he fall, he shall not be utterly cast down;
For the LORD **upholds him** with His hand.*

PSALMS 37:23-24 (NKJV), emphasis added

Perhaps desperate circumstances have left you hungry for positive change—for relief from your pain. Perhaps you have prayed
fervently, hoping at least to find God's sustaining power until you
received the change you wanted. Yet nothing's happened (that
you can see). You feel no different and your unanswered prayers
have left you disillusioned with both faith and God.

Where then does a person start digging to find the treasure of
God's supernatural, sustaining power—the power that keeps them
stable, regardless of what happens in home and country? The X
that marks the spot of God's power is found *inside the circle of His
personal plans for each of us.* In the center of His daily plans, we are
held powerfully steady through every storm. And that is true simply
and marvelously because *God's supernatural power surrounds His
plans and not ours.*

My approach to life has been radically changed in recent years
by that realization: God's power surrounds *His* plans and not mine.
I grew up hoping God would bless the plans I had for myself. And
when something went wrong, I prayed fervently (but wrongly) that

God would fix *my* plans for me. Call me crazy, but it was a new idea that God never has promised power for my plans.

And even when you ask you don't get it because your whole aim is wrong—you only want what will give **you** *pleasure.*

JAMES 4:3, emphasis added

The thrilling displays of God's supernatural power in the Bible took place because the people in those stories stepped into the ring of God's power as they pursued *His* plan—not their own.

I told you my plans and you replied. Now give me your instructions. Make me understand what **you** *want; for* **then** *I shall see your miracles.*

PSALM 119:26-27

David killed the giant Goliath because He stepped into the power that surrounded God's plan to destroy an enemy of Israel. And he did it by simply obeying his Father's request to carry food to his brothers.

Daniel was able to sleep soundly in a dark pit full of unfed lions because he stepped into the power that surrounded God's plan to reveal Himself to King Darius. And Daniel did it with his single choice to continue obeying God with his prayer time—in spite of the King's life-threatening decree. As a result, he woke up unharmed on the backs of those hungry lions. And King Darius woke up to require that all men worship Daniel's God.

Paul received visitations from God and angels. He supernaturally survived angry mobs, assassins, beatings, poisonous snakes and a shipwreck. Why? Because he, too, stepped into the power that surrounded God's plan; God's plan to get the Gospel to both Jews and Gentiles.

Even Jesus, God's own Son, did not experience supernatural power for His own plans. He tells us from the beginning that He did not come to Earth to fulfill His own plans. God's Son wielded the miraculous power that Scripture records because He, too, stepped into the power that surrounded His Father's plan to redeem us from sin and death. In John 6:38 (NKJV), we hear this truth from Jesus' own lips. He said:

> *"For I have come down from Heaven, not to do my **own will** but **the will of Him** who sent me."*
>
> emphasis added

God's power surrounds His own plan—not ours. Identifying God's voice is exciting. But even more exciting is the reality that when we identify God's voice, we also identify His plan. And when we encounter God's plan, we encounter the supernatural power that surrounds it!

In these difficult days, we need the peace and stability of God's presence and power. It can only be found inside the refuge of His plans. David said in Psalm 27:5-6:

> *There I'll be when troubles come. He will hide me. He will set me on a high rock out of reach of all my enemies. Then I will bring him sacrifices and sing his praises with much joy.*

God has never promised us smooth sailing on calm seas. In fact He warns us that—Christian or not—we *will* encounter storms, in this life. We can count on it, because Satan and his powerful forces of darkness dominate this world. While we will not escape trouble, God promises He will never leave those of us, submitted to Him, to face it alone. Alive within us, He promises to overcome every evil we encounter by redeeming the evil into a source of blessing. He will rescue us with the supernatural power we long to see.

If we are all going to face trials and tribulations, no matter what, why not face it with the unconditional guarantee of ultimate victory?

Many evils confront the [consistently] righteous; but the Lord delivers him out of them all.

PSALM 34:19 (AMP)

For a Christian, facing tribulation is such a win-win opportunity. Yet we see every day that hurting people are not running to the safe harbor a relationship with God provides. And they never will, as long as God is portrayed as someone distant and impersonal. Anyone would agree: It's hard to feel close to *distant* and *impersonal*. How can anyone be expected to love someone they don't know?

We have concluded that to know anyone, we must communicate with them. If you and I are ever going to truly know the loving God that longs to be our intimate companion, we must know how to Hear Him speaking.

God is a rewarder (Hebrews 11:6) of the people that diligently seek Him. As we learn to listen, the love that develops compels us to seek God's detailed plan for our day. We also find to our delight, that we've discovered much more than a plan. We have simultaneously encountered the X marking the spot of God's supernatural power. That task accomplished—a treasure hunter need do little more than grab their shovel of obedience and start digging!

CHAPTER 5

All We Need Is Love

You have read that people who consider themselves Christians have one of these two things: Knowledge of God or a personal relationship with Him. It's important to say that knowledge of God *is* valuable. It can produce a reverent fear that will steer us away from sin and the punishing consequences that go with it. Undoubtedly, fear of punishment does encourage obedience. No one is anxious to spend three days in the belly of a fish like Jonah did!

Yet fear of God alone does not produce devotion to God; passionate love for Him does. Plainly, love takes us to places fear can't take us. If you take a moment to consider the sacrifices you've made for those you have loved, you'll see that what I have just said is true.

Throughout your life, for the sake of love you have made endless efforts to please, spent tireless energy, given sacrificial gifts, relinquished hours of personal time, and endured sleepless nights. And at the time, you did it all with little concern for your own needs. Yet, you would struggle to do those same things today for someone you didn't really love, much less know.

Five years ago, my youngest son Micah and his wife Jordan began planning for their wedding. Out of love for them, I eagerly volunteered to help them with their wedding reception. To that end, I made 40 table centerpieces out of 600 silk flowers. I baked

1,400 cookies to ice and stack into 240 small wedding cakes, to give to guests as favors. And I finished it all just in time to pack it in the car and drive to Pennsylvania for the wedding.

That labor of love involved all of the things I just mentioned: a willingness to please, spent energy, sacrificial resources, relinquished personal time and nights with little sleep. I absolutely did it happily, with little concern for me. And yes I definitely would not do it for someone I didn't love, much less know.

Knowledge of God alone does not draw you to selfless devotion. Passionate love for God does. Passionate love draws you to the realm of sacrifice; that place where His desires are simply more important than your own. Only love for God will drive you against the headwind of your flesh's desires to fulfill the desires of His will. And fulfilling God's desires is what you were made for. That pursuit alone will satisfy your need for purpose at the deepest level; in a way serving your own plans never has. And that's a promise!

It's not hard to fall in love with God. God IS love. And we fall in love—or grow in love with Him the same way love develops with anyone—through the exchange of personal conversation. For our love relationship with God to deepen, then, we must not only talk to Him, we must know how to hear what He is saying to us. We must know how to identify God's voice.

A Walk in the Clouds

I spend a good deal of time wondering how my children will ever empty my house after I take up residence in Heaven. I'm not a hoarder but I am sentimental. I have ticket stubs from the first movie my husband and I ever saw (over 40 years ago now). I still have one curl of his dark brown hair (some of my grand-children now sport) that I cut off on a day when he was feeling brave and asked for a haircut. Now with three married children and eight grandchildren, you can just imagine how many boxes of mementoes are stuffed under my bed. Not everyone saves such things—I know. But, for the most part, that's what "lovers" do.

Not only do I have treasured evidence of my love relationships with my husband and family, I have treasured evidence of my love relationship with God. Stuck in a favorite devotional of mine is a grocery receipt: black and white proof that God's sustaining power surrounds His plan for me.

The receipt shows that a particular item I needed (when I had no income) had a sticker price of $1.97, when every other item like it was marked $6.57. I even asked a sales associate if the sticker was wrong. No one had an explanation. Here's my question: Are you *in love* with God? Is there evidence of a love relationship with Him in your life?

God is already deeply *in love* with you. Before the Earth was formed, He painted His love on the dark canvas of Calvary.

"No one has greater love—no one has shown stronger affection—than to lay down (give up) His own life for his friends."
JOHN 15:13 (AMP)

God, in the person of His Son Jesus, has loved us to death. And in keeping with His sacrifice, He wants us to feel the love He has for us. He wants us to feel the security and comfort of His great love. To that end, He has expressed His undying commitment to us, in the love letters of His Word.

Further, He has displayed His passion for us in the extravagant gestures all Creation displays. Psalm 8:3-4 (NKJV) says:

When I consider your heavens, the work of your fingers, the moon and the stars, which you have ordained, what is man that you are mindful of him, and the son of man that you visit him?

As a living person, the God of Heaven comforts me in tangible ways. One extravagant expression I will never forget took place during a spring vacation I arranged for my children, their families and myself. We stayed at a particular resort in Florida my husband had taken us to when we were all much younger. Now, there without him, I endured lonely moments as I watched other couples enjoy the resort with their children.

On the morning of our last day, the personal responsibility for getting everyone safely home settled in. As I thought about loading luggage, returning rental cars, and checking strollers, I paused to ask for God's help. Specifically, I asked Him when we should leave the pool area to pack up. Although I had an approximate idea, I knew I needed His unlimited knowledge of traffic and delays.

Upon asking Him for a specific time, I immediately heard, *2:00.* I was happy with the Holy Spirit's response. My plan would have had us leaving much earlier. God's plan gave more time to soak up last rays of cheerful sunshine.

As I sat pensively by the pool, watching my children and grandchildren play, I was suddenly blind-sided by a deep sense of despair. As objects of God's affection we should all anticipate being targets for Satan's affliction at any random time. In an attempt to hide this particular assault, I intentionally used my happy high voice to let everyone know they had ten minutes of vacation left. It was now ten minutes until two.

As I finished making my announcement, my eyes were simultaneously drawn to a small airplane skywriting some sort of message directly over our heads. Since it was Spring Break week, I assumed it was probably an advertisement for a beach party or free T-shirt. Swirling my feet in the water, I listened with interest as people in the pool guessed at what the pilot was writing.

The minutes flew by and with a few more splashes our vacation finished. At precisely 2:00, I stood up. As I did, I realized the little plane had completed the last letter of the heavenly message. Curious, I looked up into the bright sunlight to see a smiley face and beside it, these three words: "Jesus loves you."

In a matter of moments, the wind caught the message and it disappeared. The vacationers who had the chance to read the full message, were looking up at 2:00.

While some may have glanced at a frequently used cliché, I knew without doubt that God, by His Holy Spirit, was closing my emotionally tough vacation with a personal note of love for me. He wanted me to remember that I had never been alone, even for a moment. By the way, I snapped a picture of that love note. It's in my closet.

When He's not writing it in the sky, He's whispering it in my ear—*You are not alone, I am right here.*

"I will never leave you nor forsake you."

HEBREWS 13:5 (ESV)

It has been this intimate interchange with God—bringing the pages of the Bible to life—that has established my love for Him. The intimacy of my communication with God today is producing a love that surpasses any I have ever known. His love has garrisoned my heart with courage and confidence. Finally I can say and mean:

...I am convinced that nothing can ever separate us from his love.

ROMANS 8:38

His love has become personal to me because He is real to me. And God has treated me to a "walk in the clouds" on more than one occasion. One year, after some grueling weeks, my sister called and said, "Marty why don't you come out here to L.A for a week and get some rest? I'll pay for your ticket if you'll come."

Visions of sunshine and palm trees danced in my head. I thanked her for the delightful invitation. I told her that although I doubted I could leave (in light of my responsibilities and commitments) I would still ask God if I could come.

Later that busy day, after purposely making sure I had no will of my own on the matter, I asked God to reveal His will to me. In seconds, He responded. And to my real surprise, I heard, *You may go.*

Ten short days later, late at night, I was gliding silently above the clouds. The pale blue light of the full moon transformed the clouds below into one solid, glistening cushion. And above this diamond-studded cushion the clear night sky sparkled with stars. The sight took my breath away.

Warm tears kept my face turned toward the window. The tears came with the sudden understanding that the Lover of my Soul was sweeping me away to give me rest I didn't know to ask for. And in those tranquil moments on my way to the land where movies are made, a famous line came to me. With the arms of God's Presence holding me close, I whispered, "You, God, complete me."

Most of us live in the hope of being able to say those words sincerely to the earthly companion we love. The cry of every heart is: "Know me—understand me and then tell me you love what you see."

A mortal lover can meet our physical and emotional needs with a lovely dinner, physical affection, and sweet words that make us feel valuable for a time. Yet this truth remains: We are spiritual beings. And as such, only the God of Heaven can give us *a* moment where every need we have, is completely satisfied.

The next ten days in California flew by. I did get some much-needed rest. And when it was time to return to the homeland of my responsibilities, I tried to be brave.

Once again, I boarded the plane, strapped myself in, and looked out the window. I wanted to capture a few final snapshots for the photo album of my memory. Within minutes, the plane thundered down the runway. The tremendous power of the jet's engines pressed me into the seat. And there, in the middle of those exhilarating moments, the voice of the Holy Spirit spoke and said, *Now imagine the exceeding magnitude of my power.* Psalm 150:2 (NIV), says:

Praise Him for His acts of power; praise Him for his surpassing greatness.

I smiled in the comfort of my deep sense of security and settled back to stare at the clouds again. Now, at noontime, they looked very different. They were swirled in peaks like lemon tufts of cotton candy. And they glistened with yellow sunshine. Again, I marveled at God's handiwork.

Day and night alike belong to you; you made the starlight and the sun.

PSALM 74:16

In preparation for the long flight, I reached for my tiny I-pod shuffle and adjusted the earphones. Finally settled, I looked out the window and pushed the button—curious, as always, to hear which song it would randomly select to play first. And, yes, you guessed it. Once again, to let me know He was right beside me, God orchestrated another perfect moment. As I gazed out the window, I listened to a beautiful voice sing, *Lord, your name is higher than the heavens, higher than all created things, higher than hope, higher than dreams—the name of the Lord.*[3]

The love you're looking for can only be found in the arms of God. Again, knowledge of God establishes reverence for Him. But it is intimate conversation with God that establishes *love* for Him.

We must know how to hear God's voice. It's critical. Only our deep love for Him will keep us fighting to fulfill the desires of His will. And that ambition alone—fulfilling His desires—will bring the sense of 'completion' we seek. It is a loving relationship of communication with God that satisfies the human heart.

Learn to know God better and discover what He wants you to do. Next learn to put aside your own desires, ...gladly letting God have His way with you.

II PETER 1:5-6

Want to be a Hero?

If God is going to bring change to this world through you, you must possess knowledge of God's Word. But you must also possess a living love for Him or you will never be able to get past the desires of your own flesh to obey the Scripture you know.

I know people whose knowledge of the Bible is much greater than mine. Yet they disregard what they know to gratify their own desires. Hearing God's voice produces a love for God that increases your desire to serve and obey Him. And the passionate obedience of one life is all God needs to change the world. The heroes of the Bible became heroes for one reason: *They were passionately obedient to the voice of God.*

Along with increasing your desire to serve God, hearing and following the Holy Spirit's specific direction will increase the effectiveness of your service to Him. The direction coming from His divine perspective will enable you to carry the most help and hope to the greatest number of people in shortest amount of time.

As Christian soldiers we have all been given commissions in God's army of light. And we complete them successfully; burdens are lifted and needs are met, as we follow orders and get busy serving with the gifts and power God gives us. Instead of being overwhelmed by the needs we see around us, we are motivated to *yield more completely,* when we watch God's power flow through us to meet the needs we see!

The Bible provides a picture of the sin-shattering change God's power can bring to any generation when one person chooses to do the one thing Jesus did: Lovingly surrender to God the Father's direction. And, thankfully for us, the unlimited power that fueled God's plans, recorded in the Bible, exists *now* as it did *then.* That means you and I can contain this same unlimited power in our generation.

What does being a hero require? It requires a courageous heart. God is looking for courageous hearts—for Christian soldiers—to step up and step into His plan, to make His name known in this generation just as David did in his.

> *...but His own plan stands forever. His intentions are **the same** for every generation.*
>
> PSALM 33:11, emphasis added

Anyone in the mood to make a little history? Armed with your knowledge of the Bible, God wants you to be able to identify His voice so He can guide you to accomplish the Divine—courageous purposes you were preordained to accomplish—before you were born. Simply stated, He wants you to identify His voice so you can become a hero in your generation.

> *With God we shall do valiantly; it is he who will tread down our foes.*
>
> PSALM 60:12 (ESV)

CHAPTER 6

The Trace of His Grace

I f the idea of gaining direction from God's voice is new to you, don't think I'm suggesting that you've missed being directed by God. That's far from true. In His sovereignty, God has made great provision for us to be guided apart from the specific voice of His Spirit.

Five Ways God Directs Our Behavior

[1] As we have mentioned, most importantly, God directs our behavior *through His inspired written Word, the Bible.* Scripture reveals God's character and God's will. It is the supreme authority for guidance in our life on Earth.

All Scripture is God-breathed and is useful for teaching, rebuking, correcting and training in righteousness, so that the man of God may be thoroughly equipped for every good work.

II TIMOTHY 3:16-17 (NIV)

God requires that we take in the knowledge of who He is and what He requires by reading the Holy Scriptures. In coming chapters, we will learn that we must spend time reading the Bible to be able to identify God's voice.

"This Book of the Law shall not depart from your mouth, but you shall meditate in it day and night, that you may observe to do according to all that is written in it."

JOSHUA 1:8 (NKJV)

And it is important to say that, because the Bible contains the written words of God, the guidance of the Holy Spirit's voice always speaks in agreement with Scripture.

The life of Jesus is a picture of the behavior of God's righteous character. And God desires that every Christian display His same behavior. The miracle of the Bible is that, as a book, it has living power. As we read it with a sincere desire to obey, our spirit absorbs the life of God from its pages; transforming our behavior into His.

At any time throughout the day we have the opportunity to hold our behavior up to the light of Scriptural behavior and receive guidance for how we should behave in any given situation.

The integrity of the upright will guide them.

PROVERBS 11:3 (NKJV)

Simply stated, we should always be asking WWJD—What would Jesus do? God guides our behavior through the pages of Scripture.

[2] God directs our behavior *by the dictates of our conscience.* When God created man, He ordained that the compass of every soul be pointed in the direction of His Truth. To do this, He infused every soul with a conscience; a sense of right and wrong that directs our thoughts and behavior toward His truth.

Whether people use it or not, each of us has the GPS, the Guidance Placement System, of a conscience to help us make choices in a day that honor God.

> *...for **down in their hearts**, they know right from wrong. God's laws are written **within them**. Their **own conscience** accuses them.*
>
> ROMANS 2:15, emphasis added

No one—Christian or non-Christian—takes something that doesn't belong to them without knowing their behavior is wrong. Many times, in the process of paying for an item, I have received cash back that wasn't rightfully mine. My conscience has been the first line of guidance directing me to return it. We all receive God's guidance through our conscience.

[3] God directs our behavior through the *Witness of the Holy Spirit*. Once we become a Christian, by committing our lives to God, God gives us the ability to sense His Presence in and around us. We receive a distinguishable sense or witness of the Holy Spirit in our heart. In Galatians 4:6 (ESV) we read:

> *And because you are sons, God has sent the Spirit of His Son into our hearts, crying, "Abba, Father!"*

> *The Spirit Himself bears witness with our spirit that we are children of God.*
>
> ROMANS 8:16 (ESV)

I'm sure you can remember the moment when you first felt the need to commit your life to God. Since becoming a Christian, you may also remember a time when you suddenly became aware of your need to recommit your life to Him or surrender control of a problem to Him. In those moments, you became aware of His Presence and were able to respond to Him in some way. And when you obeyed, you saw results that you knew came from God. We receive guidance through the witness of the Holy Spirit.

[4] God directs our behavior through the *abilities and talents we possess.* Our interests provide guidance in God-ordained directions. God gives everyone a motivational gift. This gift provides us with motivation to serve others in a particular way within the body of Christ. Our gift determines whether we pursue jobs that require speaking skills, like that of sales and administrative positions, or jobs that require service responsibilities.

The teaching on motivational gifts is found in Romans 12:6-8. Our gifting is a "bent" toward a particular direction in life. Proverbs 22:6 (AMP) acknowledges that we have a pre-ordained bent. It says:

> *Train up a child in the way he should go, in keeping with his bent.*

In addition to spiritual gifts, God has also given us skills and talents that guide us toward His particular plans for us. God may use your ability to play an instrument to guide you to the church of His choosing. God guides us through the abilities and talents we possess.

[5] Finally, God guides our behavior through *people and circumstances.* God is the sovereign ruler over all. As such, He brings people, opportunities and circumstances into our lives to guide us to accomplish what is important to Him.

> *"For He performs [that which He has] planned for me, and of many such matters He is mindful."*
>
> JOB 23:14 (AMP)

Because of the particular people God has brought across the path of our life, many of us have been guided into a relationship with Jesus. And through others many of us have received guidance for our life that we know was God inspired.

Without counsel plans fail, but with many advisers they succeed.

PROVERBS 15:22 (ESV)

Regarding God's guidance through circumstances, we have the rich promise from Him that He will use everyday circumstances—all circumstances—good and bad—to guide us into His good plans for us.

All things *work together for good, to them that love God, to them that are called according to His purposes.*

ROMANS 8:28 (KJV), emphasis added

Surprise Plans

Every morning I acknowledge my call to God's purposes and invite Him to live out His plans through me. For that reason, few days go by that I don't experience some real spiritual adventure.

An example of God's guidance through circumstances took place one day as I fought for some uninterrupted time to write. I was concerned I wasn't going to get the time I needed to finish a message I was to give in days. Crunch time. And I felt the pressure. I was typing furiously when the doorbell rang.

Through the circumstance of my Internet service being down, a young man from the cable company stood smiling at my door. I worked to hide my frustration. He wasn't scheduled to come for several days. But now that he was here, I smiled, directed him to the computer I *had* been using, and asked him if he needed me for any further reason. To my surprise, he said, "Well it's always nice to have company." I knew God was changing up my plans for the afternoon.

Over the next hour, I talked to him about his relationship with God. He shared that his parents were divorced before he was born. But he went on to say that his mother had taken him to church three times a week. Now, standing before me, it was quite apparent he had replaced his church attendance with other activities.

God directed my words. I gave him Biblical advice and even some stern warnings. I was very aware that God, through me, was seeking to restore his spiritual hunger. The entire time I talked, he stood completely still, listening intently, staring straight at me.

At one point, he shared his desire to help bring change to poverty-stricken countries of the world. And after he did, I reminded him that he would need God's power to accomplish a dream that size. Sensing God's purpose had been accomplished, I drew my counsel to a close and thanked him for getting my Internet service back up.

He left and I returned to my computer. I tried to pick up where I left off but I kept being distracted with wondering whether or not my son and his wife had successfully made some flight connections. Knowing I would have to settle the question, I decided to call the airlines and find out.

I dialed the number and a friendly representative answered. She told me that my kids did make their flight and that it was on time. I made one closing comment and the next thing I know—another heart was pouring out her life story. I tried to process what was happening. At this rate, I wondered how God ever intended for me to finish writing.

Nevertheless, sensing God had clearly orchestrated this circumstance too, I obediently listened to this woman with compassion. The kind voice shared that she was divorced from an alcoholic husband, had raised a stepdaughter alone, and was now in a long-distance relationship with a man. Startled by her openness, I felt like I was listening to the woman at the well. The Holy Spirit used that thought to make it clear to me that He and I were doing exactly that.

The mental picture of Jesus talking with the woman at the well (John 4) made me realize the importance of this woman to God. Purposefully, then, I settled my anxious thoughts and took some time to carefully explain that God alone was the answer for the problems she faced. She responded with gratefulness and when it was time, I thanked her for the talk and her information and closed this second conversation.

The rest of my day proceeded just as busily. Yet, God's voice assured me that because I had yielded to His surprise plans, He would take care of the ones that concerned me.

The next day, my thoughts came so quickly that I finished my writing in half the expected time. We receive guidance into God's good plans for our day through people and circumstances.

God has made it possible for us to identify His plan in a variety of wonderful ways. And when we do, we are swept into the force field of power that surrounds them. There we witness the miraculous daily victories that accompany His plans!

CHAPTER 7

Your Free Gift With Salvation The Guidance of His Voice

Not only is my bedroom stuffed with mementos, I have quite the collection of free gifts to show for all the make-up I've purchased over the years. They've actually come in quite handy during these lean economic times. But nothing on Earth compares to the extra free gift God has for us; the gift that comes with His purchased price for our salvation.

That gift is the guidance of His Voice. When you can identify God is speaking, you can have everyday guidance in the smallest details of life. God wants you to be able to hear His voice speaking to you so He can personally address your needs and burdens. More importantly, He wants you to recognize His voice so that you can easily find and remain on His path of purpose for you.

> *The Lord says, "I will guide you along the best pathway for your life. I will **advise** you and watch over you."*
>
> PSALM 32:8, emphasis added

Salvation is the greatest gift any person can ever receive. I hope you have experienced being saved from eternal death; the penalty for your personal sins. Anyone can be supernaturally, spectacularly changed by making the single decision to ask Jesus—who paid the price for sin with His own blood—to possess them and take control of their life.

Once we make the decision to commit our life to God, we have learned that God sends His own Holy Spirit to dwell in us. Further, He gives us the ability to physically sense the Presence of His Spirit as proof we have been redeemed from the penalty of our own sin. And it is this gift of His Presence that makes it possible for us to hear His Voice.

I was in the fourth grade when I clearly remember first having the desire to hear God speak. Looking back, I understand that God placed that desire in me before I was born—just as He has placed desires in your heart that He intends to fulfill.

As a preacher's daughter, I grew up listening to the captivating stories of missionaries who served God in distant lands. It's interesting now to consider that while Satan was using their stories of sacrifice to create fear of trusting God, God was using their testimonies to inspire me to accomplish His Divine purpose.

Every time I heard a missionary say, "God spoke to me and said," my desire to hear God's Voice grew stronger. I remember wondering if it was wrong to want God to speak to me. Somehow it seemed like hearing God's voice was a privilege regular people didn't deserve.

Over the years, it's become apparent that I'm not the only one who has ever felt that way. As I have taught on the subject of hearing God's voice, a variety of people have approached me and said some variation of, "I know that God speaks to some people but I can't hear Him speaking. He doesn't speak to me."

God is no respecter of persons. He speaks to everyone. Can you imagine any person truly "in love" *not* wanting to talk to the person they were in love with? God is in love with you. As the lover of your soul, He longs to speak to you, to reveal Himself to you. He wants to redeem every misery of your past and fulfill His sweetest dreams for your future.

Concerning God, I have made the point that Christians have one of two things: knowledge of Him, or a real relationship with Him. That reality is hard to dispute. We all know the difference between those with whom we are only generally acquainted and those with whom we have a genuine relationship.

All Christians have the ability to sense God's Presence. But not all Christians experience the daily exchange of conversation that results from being in genuine relationship with Him. And, again, communication is the lifeblood of relationship. You can't know and love someone without it.

How can anyone expect to develop a relationship with God if they only communicate with Him during the personal prayer time of daily devotions? I believe this single reality explains why so many Christians could admit that they don't feel like they really know God. And, as I have said in a previous chapter, it's hard to live for the desires of someone you don't really know.

Before God revealed Himself to me, my faith was a collection of Biblical truths I reverenced and tried to obey. God was a subject to be studied. And the Bible was a power-filled puzzle. I plodded along the road of Christian duty, assuming that if I studied the Bible long enough, I would learn how to work the promises of Scripture to get the power I needed to accomplish my plans. In chapter four we learned that experiencing God's power requires that we be in step with *His* plan. And again, *we will resist exchanging our plans for His if we are not in love with God.* The supernatural encounters with God for which we long come to those who love Him. In John 14:23, Jesus said:

"I will only reveal myself to those who love me and obey me."

How, When and Where?

In the last chapter I listed five ways we identify God's direction for our daily behavior, apart from recognizing the voice of the Holy Spirit. We learned that God directs us through:

+ His Written Word, the Bible

+ Our conscience

+ The witness of the Holy Spirit

+ Our abilities and talents

+ People and circumstances

You may be wondering, again, why it's even necessary to identify the Holy Spirit's voice, since we already have these other ways for God to direct our behavior. Can't we just rely on circumstances to reveal what God wants us to do in a day?

We could if God was the *only one* who orchestrated our circumstances. But that's not the case. Some of the circumstances we encounter are set up by spirits of darkness to stop us from accomplishing God's plan.

It's easy to say we will just rely on the Bible to show us God's will for our behavior. The last part of II Timothy 3:17 assures us that Scripture equips us for every good work. The Bible absolutely paints a clear picture of the righteous character of God we are to model.

But we still need to know how, when, and where God wants to demonstrate this behavior through us. If we disregard the need for the direction of God's Spirit—relying on His written Word alone to provide personal direction—how will we know what to do and when to do it? As wrapped up as we are in our own problems, how will we know to stop and devote time to the needs of others? Ask yourself how readily you respond to the idea of making a simple phone call to encourage someone.

Apart from the clear direction of the Holy Spirit, how will we know when it is right to speak and when it is right to listen? Ecclesiastes 3:7 (AMP) says there is a time to keep silent and a time to speak.

Consider this direction from the Word of God regarding the necessity of confronting others:

> ...*warn (admonish, urge, and encourage) one another every day, as long as it is called Today, that none of you may be hardened by the deceitfulness of sin...*
>
> HEBREWS 3:13 (AMP)

Yet James 1:19 says:

> *Dear brothers, don't ever forget that it is best to listen much, speak little, and not become angry;*

How will we know when we should confront an offense and when we should disregard it?

> *"Moreover, if your brother sins against you, go and tell him his fault between you and him alone."*
>
> MATTHEW 18:15 (NKJV)

Yet in Proverbs 19:11 (NKJV), we read:

> *The discretion of a man makes him slow to anger, And his glory is to overlook a transgression.*

How will we know when to give money away and when to invest? In Mark 12:44, (NLT) Jesus observed the widow's offering and said:

> *"She, poor as she is, has given everything she had to live on."*

On the other hand, in Matthew 25:21 (NLT), Jesus tells the parable of the master who commended his servant for investing his money responsibly, saying:

"Well done, my good and faithful servant. You have been faithful in handling this small amount..."

Again, we need to be able to identify the voice of the Holy Spirit's direction so that we will know what to do, where it should be done, how to go about it, and when to do it. An everyday situation that illustrates this sincere need for specific direction took place when I was in a grocery store parking lot.

One day, as I slowly backed out of a very tight parking space, a panicked woman's face startled me. From the front of my car, she thrust her hand forward and loudly began yelling, "Stop!"

Instinctively—I stopped. As she approached the passenger's side of my car, I had the presence of mind to lower my window only slightly. And, once I did, she began pleading with me to give her whatever change I had. She kept repeating that she just needed a little gas money to get home.

I stared at the young child the woman was holding. The little girl's face was expressionless and dirty. Instantly, I began asking God for wisdom.

For the Lord grants wisdom! His every word is a treasure...
He grants good sense to his saints. He is their shield, protecting
them and guarding their pathway. He shows how to...find
the right decision every time.
PROVERBS 2:6-9

As she continued her pleading, I thought about the dangerous scams people practice in large parking lots. And I thought about the reality that the $25 in my wallet had to carry me for the week due to my own lack of income.

Moments were passing and I had to make a decision. Did God want me to give money away to this woman or carefully manage what I had left? In seconds that seemed like hours I *reasoned* that, regardless of whether or not she was really in need, I could give her my $5 bill, as precious as it was.

As I opened my wallet, I clearly heard, **Give her the $20 bill.** Startled again, I painfully extended the $20 towards her. The moment I did, she snatched it from me, mumbled, "God bless you," and ran off toward the store—not back toward the car that needed the gas.

As I slowly pulled away, I struggled. Had I heard God's voice? Did I do what He wanted me to do? Was He pleased that I had given that woman my $20 bill? Or was He displeased? Had I been weak and foolish? Before I could even reach the edge of the parking lot, God responded. The Holy Spirit confirmed the direction of His voice and erased my anxiety with these words from Matthew 25:40 (KJV). I clearly heard:

"Inasmuch as ye have done it unto one of the least of these my brethren, ye have done it unto me."

I smiled and headed home; confident God would meet my needs, just as He had used me to meet hers.

When you walk about, they will guide you; when you sleep, they will watch over you; and when you awake, they will talk to you. For the commandment is a lamp, and the teaching is light;
PROVERBS 6:22-23 (NASB)

God's written Word speaks to us, providing a lamp of direction that is wholly sufficient to lead us on the path of living righteously. The questions are, "How?" "Where?" "When?" In what specific ways, each day, does God want to use our righteous behavior to accomplish what's important to Him? God has made provision for each of us to know how to accomplish what is important to Him by giving us His Holy Spirit as a guide.

For as many as are led by the Spirit of God, they are the sons of God.

ROMANS 8:14 (KJV)

New Clothes

Our faith is a faith to follow. By definition, Christians are followers of Jesus Christ. Jesus said in John 12:26 (NKJV):

"If anyone serves Me, let him follow Me; and where I am, there My servant will be also…"

Yet, in the admonition to follow Jesus, God intends that we do far more than copy the behavior Jesus displayed on Earth. He intends that we literally put Jesus on and allow Him—in Spirit—to continue living out His desires, on Earth, through us.

And all who have been united with Christ…have put on Christ, like putting on new clothes.

GALATIANS 3:27

Why has God made this possible?

…so that the life of Jesus may also be seen in our bodies.

II CORINTHIANS 4:10 (NLT)

God wants people to see Jesus when they look at us. Therefore He has made provision for us to put Jesus on by giving us the ability to house His very Spirit in our own body.

He has given us of His Spirit.

I JOHN 4:13 (KJV)

And because He has, we can begin the journey of being able to be:

...filled with all the fullness of God.

EPHESIANS 3:19 (NKJV)

Again, we have been given this privilege so that *God's own Spirit* can guide us to accomplish *His own personal desires*; to such an extent that Jesus said, in Matthew 10:40:

"Those who welcome you are welcoming Me."

As vessels filled with God, then, Romans 6:13 tells us that we are to yield ourselves to God's control so that we can personally be used as instruments of righteousness. Needless to say, with as many needs as there are in the world, God has plenty of righteous purposes to accomplish in a day. And since God has declared that we are to yield ourselves to His control, it is certainly necessary for us to know *when* we have! How much of the activity of your day is under the Holy Spirit's control? Notice I didn't say, "How much of your day is lived free from willful sin?" There's a big difference.

The ability to identify God's voice of direction allows us to know that we have given Him control. The following verses make it clear that it is possible to hear what God is saying to us.

"He who is of God hears God's words..."

JOHN 8:47 (NKJV)

"...everyone who is of the truth hears My voice."

JOHN 18:37 (NKJV)

If you want to know what God wants you to do, ask Him and He will gladly tell you, for He is always ready to give a bountiful supply of wisdom to all who ask Him.

JAMES 1:5-8

It is God's desire that we allow Jesus, through our mortal bodies, to continue doing what He did when He walked the Earth: Reflect God, in word and deed, so that people who do not know Him will be drawn to Him by seeing God in us.

Because God, alone, knows the thoughts of every man, only God can tell us how to use the gifts He has given us to draw the lost of this world to Himself. And their number is far too great for God to allow us to wander through a day relying on circumstances alone to get the job done. God has detailed plans to accomplish detailed purposes. And He intends that we be able to identify His plans in the daily events of life.

I have said before, I have no idea how to reach this world God loves, day by day. But He knows exactly how to do it; through everyday people, like you and me, who make the choice to "put Jesus on" and follow the direction of His Spirit—God's free gift!

CHAPTER 8

A Biblical Basis

If this is the first time you have heard it is possible to hear God's voice speaking, to direct the details of your life, you can find the scriptural basis for this truth in two familiar verses: Proverbs 3:5 & 6. These verses happen to be very familiar to me. I quickly selected them the day my homeroom teacher asked seniors to turn in their favorite passage. I've got to smile at the way God knits a plan together.

> *Trust in the LORD with all your heart; and lean not on your own understanding.* ***In all your ways****, acknowledge Him and He will* ***direct*** *your path.*
>
> PROVERBS 3:5-6 (NKJV), emphasis added

These verses alert us to the spiritual reality that there are two "voices" that seek to guide Christians in making daily decisions. The first one is the voice of our own human understanding—our own self-thoughts. In Romans 8:6-8 (AMP), we read that the voice of our human understanding is also referred to as the *Mind of the Flesh.*

The desires of our flesh make it easy for us to create plans without consulting God. If you are like me, after our plans are well underway, it often occurs to us that we never stopped initially to consider what God wanted. At that point, many of us typically utter a quick prayer asking God to bless what we've done in an effort to ensure our own plan's success.

Making decisions on the basis of our own desires and limited knowledge is called leaning on our own understanding. And in Proverbs 3:5 God warns us we're not to do it.

The other voice, that speaks to guide our daily decisions, is of course the voice of the Holy Spirit. In I Corinthians 2:16 we read that God's revealed will, through His Holy Spirit, is referred to as the *Mind of Christ*. This book has been written to help you *distinguish the difference between the two*; the Mind of the Flesh and the Mind of Christ.

God can warn us not to lean on our own understanding in Proverbs 3:5 because Proverbs 3:6 tells us His understanding—His guidance—*is available* for *all* of our ways.

Let's dissect verse 6: "In all your ways…" The word "ways" in Hebrew refers to the literal roads we take to get physically from one place to another. That means, then, that God wants us to become aware of Him in all of our literal ways because He has guidance available for all our literal ways.

Next, "In all your ways, acknowledge Him…" "Acknowledge" in Hebrew, is *yaw-dah*. It means, learn to know—find out and discern God.

We've learned from Proverbs 3:6 then, that in all of our physical ways, we are to seek God out; to discern what He would have us do.

When we listen for the voice of God's direction, that is exactly what we are doing: acknowledging His Presence—seeking to discern what He would have us do—in all of our ways.

The exciting part of verse six is the last part. It contains a commitment from God. If we choose to become aware of Him—to discern what He would have us do—in all we do, the verse closes with the words, "He shall direct thy path."

The literal meaning is, "He will show you what to do." The Hebrew translation reads: "He Himself shall make the paths straight—removing all obstacles out of the way."

In the face of adversarial defiance, we have nothing to fear. God has declared that He will go before us and make a way for His will to be done.

We have learned that the plans and purposes of God are surrounded by a force field of His power. If you are confronting constant chaos in the daily living that takes you from one place to another, it may be that your day and your ways are still under your own control. If you and I want to experience the stabilizing power of God in our daily circumstances and the peace of mind that goes with it, we must surrender our plans to God's control.

Commit your actions to the Lord and your plans will succeed.
PROVERBS 16:3 (NLT)

Sound Principles—Not Sensations

Most Christians would readily agree with this statement: God has given us life on Earth to accomplish His will. And yet my observation, over a lifetime of church attendance, makes it clear that many Christians practically interpret "doing God's will" to mean, "doing anything I want" as long as I refrain from breaking the Ten Commandments. They regard the concept of receiving God's guidance to do His will far more figuratively than literally.

When God tells us in Romans 6:13 that we are to yield control of ourselves to Him, He means it—literally. And since He requires that we yield control to Him, we've said that it's critical that we know how He directs us. If we don't know how He directs us, how will we know whether or not we have yielded control to Him?

In previous chapters, we have learned that God guides us through the principles of His Inspired Written Word.

He gave you His rules for daily life so you would know what He wanted you to do.

ROMANS 9:4B

We have also learned He uses the voice of His own Spirit–the Holy Spirit—to tell us how, when, and where to use the righteous character His Written Word has forged in us.

Whenever I have questions about a controversial subject or need more understanding for a particular subject, I head for my study Bibles. One of my favorites is by John MacArthur. Years ago, as I studied the subject of guidance by the Holy Spirit, I read his study notes on Romans 8:14 (NKJV). That verse says:

For as many as are led by the Spirit of God, these are the sons of God.

MacArthur's study notes on this verse say that God does not lead us with personal, inward, mental impressions. His notes say that God leads us outwardly through the principles of His Word and through the orchestration of circumstances. [4]

All of that is true. The Spirit of God does not lead us with personal, inward, mental impressions. The dictionary tells us that mental impressions are sensations, feelings or strong effects made on our intellect.

First, I am not suggesting that anyone ever seek to be led by impressions, sensations or feelings. Rather, I am emphatically stating that all of us should seek to be led by *clear, sound thoughts that prompt us to take action consistent with the principles of God's Written Word.*

Secondly, I am not suggesting that anyone take action based on the personal deductions of their intellect. The thoughts we need to capture are not generated by our intellect. We are seeking to capture thoughts generated by God. These thoughts come to us apart from the desires of our own will and idea of goodness.

It's important to say here, (as we learn to identify the source of our thoughts) that there's a great difference between working to generate good thoughts with our intellect and identifying the righteous thoughts of God sent to our spirit.

We can't think-up God's will. God's will has to be *revealed* to us by His Own Spirit. *The goal is to learn how to capture thoughts generated by God's Spirit.* We want to learn how to stop, consider, and then obey the clear, persistent thoughts that result in God-honoring behavior. As I have already acknowledged, God does lead us through the principles of His Word and through the orchestration of circumstances.

What was not mentioned in MacArthur's study notes is the reality that all "leading" to take *any* action begins inwardly. It begins inwardly with a thought. Before we ever act on any outward principle of Scripture, like that of putting money in an offering plate, the inward thought to do it comes first.

Let me be perfectly clear. My goal is to help you identify and walk out the behavior of God-given directives that prompt you to action. The word "prompt" does not suggest an uncontrollable knee-jerk response to a fleshly desire. The word prompt means both—move to action and remember. God will prompt or "move us to action" with new thoughts to direct the specific desires of His will. And God will prompt or bring to our remembrance (our conscious mind) a truth committed to memory to direct the desires of His will.

The Example of Jesus

Hebrews 2:14 explains that Jesus was fully man as well as fully God. Being fully man, even Jesus needed the direction of God's Spirit. And He received it in a variety of ways. To respond correctly to Satan in the wilderness, Jesus drew direction directly from the written *Word of God.* He quoted it to Satan. Jesus was directed by the *circumstances* of His life, as well. Out of the circumstance of need for more wine at a wedding in Cana, Jesus performed His first miracle.

However, in addition to receiving direction through the written Word of God and through the circumstances of His life, Jesus also received guidance directly from the Holy Spirit. Luke 4:1 says:

Then Jesus, full of the Holy Spirit, left the Jordan River, being urged by the Spirit, out into the barren wastelands.

Throughout the New Testament, we read evidence of other believers receiving specific daily direction from the Holy Spirit. In Acts 23:11 the Lord told Paul he was to go to Rome. In I Corinthians 4:19 Paul expressed this ability to receive daily direction from God. He said:

I will come, and soon, if the Lord will let me.

Further, in I Corinthians 7:17 Paul speaks of marrying or not marrying in accordance with God's individual direction.

How Does it Work?

Let's talk, then, about how a person actually receives a direct communication from God. First, the Bible tells us we are all born with a receiver for hearing His voice. That receiver is our spirit.

The Lord...forms the spirit of man within him.
ZECHARIAH 12:1 (NKJV)

It is your spirit that enables you to worship God and communicate with Him.

God is a Spirit: and they that worship him must worship him in spirit and in truth.
JOHN 4:24 (KJV)

Although we are all born with a spirit, Ephesians 2:5 explains that until a person purposefully commits their life to Jesus, their spirit—their receiver—is dead. The sin in them blocks reception. They cannot access God.

> *But the natural man does not receive the things of the Spirit of God...nor can he know them, because they are spiritually discerned.*
>
> I CORINTHIANS 2:14 (NKJV)

We can liken our spirit to a cell phone. At birth, we all receive a phone. However, it must be activated to receive a signal. Salvation provides that activation. Salvation is the transformation of our sin nature by God's power. It follows a prayer of repentance for personal sin where in we ask God to accept Jesus Christ's death on the cross as payment for our personal sin and indwell us—possess us—with His own Holy Spirit.

You and I receive the Holy Spirit the moment we pray this prayer; receiving God's free gift of Salvation.

> *But you have received the Holy Spirit and He lives within you...*
>
> I JOHN 2:27 (NLT)

And the first thing God does, when His Spirit takes up residence in you, is activate your spirit.

> *And you He made alive who were dead in trespasses and sins...*
>
> EPHESIANS 2:1 (NKJV)

Now that the lines are open and your spirit is ready to receive direct communication from God as He chooses, His desires travel from His heart to yours in these three steps:

First, God the Father speaks His will—His desires for you at the time—to the Holy Spirit. Speaking of the Holy Spirit Jesus said:

*...for He will not speak on His own authority, but whatever
He hears He will speak.*

JOHN 16:13 (NKJV)

Next, the Holy Spirit, who now lives in you, speaks the will of
God that He has heard to your spirit.

*And God has actually given us His Spirit to tell us about the
wonderful free gifts of grace and blessing that God has given us.*

I CORINTHIANS 2:12

And finally, that knowledge (imparted by the Holy Spirit to your
spirit) goes from your spirit to your mind as a conscious thought.

*For who has known or understood the mind (the counsels and
purposes) of the Lord so as to guide and instruct [Him] and
give Him knowledge? But we have the mind of Christ, the
Messiah, and do hold the thoughts (feelings and purposes) of
His heart.*

I CORINTHIANS 2:16 (AMP)

And what is the wonderful result? God's very own thoughts are
now directing your behavior to carry out the action He desires. You
are walking in the Spirit.

As mortal human beings we have been given the unfathomable
opportunity to walk out God's personal will on Earth. How eagerly
God must wait, each morning, for you and I to recognize and obey
His voice. It is our obedience that gives Him hands and feet to bless
and redeem the world He so desperately loves.

*God has said of you, "I will live in them and walk among
them."*

II CORINTHIANS 6:16

CHAPTER 9

The Fount of True Faith

People are quite intrigued when I share my stories about receiving direction from God. They enjoy hearing the remarkable results that come from obeying what I hear. In a way, they seem grateful to have new information to add to the "collection of supernatural evidence" they keep that assures them God is real.

Needless to say, we all like to have evidence of God's existence, to get us through times of doubt. We hope the supernatural events we hear about, will serve as "Spiritual Miracle Grow" for our faith. Everybody likes to hear stories that involve the miraculous.

I must admit the results of my obedience to God's voice have produced some pretty amazing evidence of His existence. If you have picked up this book in the hope of receiving strength for your personal faith, you may be anticipating that it will happen as you read of such miraculous accounts.

Perhaps you are hoping I will tell you, that listening to God's voice has saved my life. Hope no more. It has. The persistent voice of God prompted me to ask my doctor a question just as he was leaving the examination room. And that single question gave him the chance to diagnose malignant Melanoma before it became terminal for me.

Perhaps you're hoping to find out that obedience to God's voice has produced financial miracles in my life. It has. As a result of my obedience in running one unpleasant errand, I came home $2,500 richer. And I received that money when I had a zero balance in my checking account.

At the feet of the Holy Spirit I have learned many life-changing lessons. One He taught me in particular has to do with this very subject—the subject of where faith comes from. What did He teach me? Just this: *That faith in God does not come as a result of observing miracles.*

If it did, I would certainly fill the remainder of this book with the details of the most miraculous results I have experienced. Although the miraculous results, like the ones I just mentioned, provide us with tremendous evidence of God's existence, they do not produce the faith in God we all long for. In case you're scratching your head right about now, let's talk about why that's true.

The passage of Scripture the Holy Spirit used to teach me this lesson was John 6:22-40. In this passage, Jesus is talking with a group of doubters. Specifically the people he is talking with were part of the very crowd of 5000 Jesus had just fed, the day before, with a single child's lunch. The provision of that lunch, alone, should have been amazing evidence enough, for these people that Jesus was the Messiah.

Yet, they obviously disregarded that small feat, and were now asking Him to do more miracles to prove He was the Messiah. In verses 30 and 31, we read their words. They said:

"You must show us more miracles if you want us to believe you are the Messiah. Give us free bread every day, like our fathers had while they journeyed through the wilderness!"

And to add insult to injury, they were asking Him for more evidence right after concluding He had been physically transported from the other side of the sea, without a boat! What exasperation and discouragement the Lord must have felt in those moments.

If you're a parent, perhaps remembering an ungrateful remark from a much-loved son or daughter will help you identify with the pain Jesus must have been feeling. You may remember a time when you received a smart comment from the young voice you'd die for. You know—a voice that accused you of not caring for them—as they picked up the phone, you purchased for them, grabbed the keys to their new car and slammed the door by the kitchen table where their dinner was sitting? In such moments there's little to say. Sometimes shaking your head is all you can do. In John 6:36, we read what Jesus said:

"...you haven't believed even though you have seen me."

Confronted with the same doubt, Mark 8:12 says:

He sighed deeply...

After all that these, much loved, people had seen Jesus do, with their own eyes, many still refused to believe He was who He said He was.

"...seeing they do not see, and hearing they do not hear, nor do they understand."
MATTHEW 13:13 (NKJV)

Clearly these particular people did not experience faith in God as a result of seeing miracles. Consequently the Bible tells us Jesus refused to do any more. He knew it would have no affect on their faith.

To underscore the point, if faith came as a result of witnessing miracles, Jesus never would have been arrested and crucified by the particular soldiers that tied His hands, in the garden of Gethsemane and led Him away. When they saw Jesus pick up and reattach the ear of their comrade, Peter had sliced off with his sword, they certainly would have bowed before Him in saving faith.

"Though you watch and watch as I perform my miracles, still you won't know what they mean."

ISAIAH 6:9

Bringing it closer home, perhaps you've heard, as I have, that currently, in some foreign countries, missionaries are watching the power of God raise people from the dead. If you have heard that account or other such accounts, may I ask you, what specific difference has that awareness made in your personal walk with God?

If witnessing the miraculous does not generate faith, where, then, does faith come from? The Bible says in Romans 10:17 (KJV), that:

Faith cometh by hearing and hearing by the Word of God.

In other words, faith comes from "taking in"—from "knowing" the Word of God. It comes from knowing the written Word and most importantly it comes from knowing the living Word of God, Jesus Christ. Again, God did not give us the Bible so that His words could be known. He gave us the Bible so that *He* could be known.

The Holy Spirit made it clear to me that genuine faith—the kind that withstands every test of doubt—comes from knowing Jesus, the Living Word of God. *It is an intimate relationship of communication with Him that will erase your doubt.*

My Mom and I are best of friends. She knows me well and I know her well. As a matter of fact I know her so well, it would be impossible for anyone to create doubts in my heart about her character and her love for me.

When you know Jesus intimately, the same is true. As you spend time communicating with Him throughout the day, your knowledge of Him, coupled with His returned assurance of love for you, keeps Satan from being able to create doubts in your heart about His Character or love for you.

To have powerful, unwavering faith in God you must have more than a knowledge of the miracles He performs. You must *know Him*. Hearing God's voice does not increase your faith by giving you supernatural evidence that God is real. Hearing God's voice increases your faith by establishing a relationship of intimacy with God the Father and Jesus His Son.

The results of the accounts of listening to God's voice in the next chapters are not shared to give you 'over-the-top' evidence of God's existence. They are shared to give you examples of the daily interchange of conversation that make up *the fiber of a love relationship with Jesus*. That fiber, in turn, is what establishes unwavering faith in a human heart.

I want to admit that along my own road of obedience, I have often wondered what possible purpose could come from obeying the detailed direction God has given me. It has often seemed insignificant in the grand scheme of things. Yet I have learned that a life that brings change, in the world, is made up of days. And days are made up of hours and hours are made up of ordinary events.

Recently, God's voice directed me to turn into a grocery store parking lot. It seemed odd to me since I wasn't in need of much. I was almost through the store when I received a text message from my daughter-in-law. She had her two sons and newborn daughter in the car. She wanted to know if she could bring them by the house, for me to watch briefly, while she picked up a few grocery items she was desperate for.

It was fun to be able to tell her I was in a grocery store at that very moment. And it was even more fun to find out that she was a block away from the grocery store I was in. I was able to grab the items she needed and walk them to the door just as she pulled up. By being in God's spot at God's time, an ordinary event became extraordinary for both of us. She smiled as she told me how "perfectly" things worked out for her. And I smiled to be part of the blessing that accompanies hearing and obeying God's voice.

The very next day, I was leaving my doctor's office, when it occurred to me that I could take lunch to my daughter and her children before I picked up the medicine my doctor had prescribed. As I began thinking about what they might like to eat, I heard, *No, go directly to the drug store.*

Quite honestly I thought it was odd that God was not in favor of me buying my children lunch. Nonetheless, I obeyed and headed for the drug store.

Once again, while cruising the aisles, I received a text. It was my daughter, asking where I was. When I told her, she asked if I would be willing to pick up a prescription for my granddaughter that was waiting at that same drug store. I smiled. How about that? I got to take them a much needed prescription and lunch!

The results of our obedience, large and small exist to achieve God's desired ends. And He alone knows how to turn the ordinary events of our life into purposeful opportunities that accomplish His goals of service, growth and salvation for those He loves.

Over everything, it's ordinary events that provide God with the opportunity to achieve the desired end He cares about most—conforming His own to His image. As we spend the large amounts of time—ordinary events consume—listening for the direction of the Holy Spirit of God, we will indeed wake up to find that gradually and wonderfully, we are starting to look like our lover! Perhaps you've noticed that phenomenon in earthly lovers. As a result of spending their lives together—some actually do look alike!

As we go about our God directed, daily routines we see that our love for Him increases. As our love increases, we see that our faith in Him increases. As our faith increases, we see that our obedience to God increases. And as our obedience increases, we find that the power of God through us increases! Jesus is the Fount of every blessing. True Faith flows from knowing Him.

CHAPTER 10

A Two-Day Measure for Your Learning Pleasure!

Nine years ago now, at God's direction, some Christian friends and family members of mine, helped me begin a ministry, known as "Jesus First—Wives Club." JFWC functioned as a non-profit women's ministry whose particular focus was strengthening the Christian home. Needless to say, the problems that confront the Christian home and marriage, today, are great. And they are as varied as we are. Yet God is more than able to give us wisdom for tackling each one. A paraphrase of Hebrews 4:13-15, says:

He knows about everyone, everywhere. Everything about us is bare and wide open to the all-seeing eyes of our living God; but Jesus the Son of God is our great High Priest who has gone to Heaven itself to help us; therefore let us never stop trusting him. This High Priest of ours understands our weaknesses...

The ministry existed for five plus years to direct those who came, to the one love that satisfies and the only hope that does not disappoint. And we sought to accomplish those objectives by teaching the women how to transfer their human hope—for a love filled life—to Jesus Christ. Psalm 33:22 says:

Yes Lord, let your constant love surround us, for our hopes are in you alone.

We told those who came that if they were married, our goal was to equip them to increase the demonstration of love in their home and marriage. If they were formerly married, our goal was to give them the opportunity to know Jesus as their husband; giving Him the freedom to restore their broken relationship. If they were single, we sought to help them learn how to enjoy being a wife to Jesus first.

Over the six years, we ministered to approximately 4,000 women, once a month with a message and meal. And as a token of God's love, we always sent them home with a small gift. God enabled us to operate the ministry at no cost to those who attended. We were graciously supported by donations.

As we have learned, God has specific ordained purposes for each of us. And He has uniquely designed us to accomplish them. I took this responsibility God called me to very seriously.

…we talk about Christ to all who will listen, warning them and teaching them as well as we know how. We want to be able to present each one to God, perfect because of what Christ has done for each of them. This is my work, and I can do it only because Christ's mighty energy is at work within me.

COLOSSIANS 1:28-29

When God's daily plan for me involved this ministry responsibility, I did find His direction to me ratcheted up a notch!

To illustrate the truth that God will definitely direct our path when we acknowledge Him—making a way for His glorious will to be done, I thought you might enjoy reading a two-day account of some ordinary events that became extraordinary. We experienced God's power because we simply followed the voice of His direction and as a result—encountered the power that surrounds His plan.

The stage was set for the events of these two December days, in September of that year. And it all started, as I walked through a store and began shopping for the small gifts we would give out at the Christmas meeting for Jesus First Wives Club.

Because our staff was small, our preparation required a good deal of planning in advance. On this particular day, three months in advance, I was trying to determine how many attendees I should prepare for. Knowing our average attendance at the time was 60 women, and the largest crowd ever was 99, I asked God how many women I should buy gifts for. And within moments I heard the number, *125*. Although that number seemed comparatively high, I got busy and purchased a variety of items for gift baskets in lots of 125 and left the store.

Three months later, in December, two days before our Christmas meeting, volunteers came to my home to assemble the baskets. While we were busy working, I casually asked my friend, who was in charge of registration, how many women had registered. She answered, "55". I was stunned.

Immediately, someone else spoke up and asked, "Then how many baskets should we make, since we have double the amount of gifts we need?"

Somewhat embarrassed, I considered again what I knew God had said and weakly replied, "125". When the last bow was tied on the last basket, everyone headed home.

The following morning I received a phone call from my daughter, Christy, who served as our administrative director and also helped prepare the meals. She was calling to tell me that when she tried to preheat her oven to bake the pineapple chicken, we would be serving for dinner at the event, she realized her stove had stopped working. She had already called the repair service and was regretfully informed they had no appointments available for the rest of the day.

Quite discouraged, we spent the next half hour trying to figure out how and where she could bake the chicken. After discussing all the options, she decided she would take the 20 pounds of chicken and her three small children to my daughter-in-law's house. Christy knew Amy would gladly volunteer her kitchen.

I couldn't bake the chicken because I was baking the gigantic birthday cake for Jesus we served each Christmas for dessert. Feeling terrible that she was faced with such a monumental task, I told her that I would pray that God would send help somehow and hung up the phone.

The instant I hung up, I heard, *Call her back now and pray with her—on the phone.* Although I clearly heard what I heard, I hesitated to obey, *reasoning* my phone call would be an annoyance in the middle of getting the children ready to go.

Firmly, God repeated His instruction to me and I obeyed. As we prayed together, over the phone, I asked God to open a way through this Red Sea of opposition we were facing.

Just as I said, "Amen," she asked me to hang on; she was getting another call. At that moment, I knew God was in the process of answering our prayer. When my daughter came back on the line, she excitedly confirmed that the call was from the repair company. They told her they had just received two cancellations and would be at her house in 10 minutes. Within the hour, her stove was back in business.

Opposition continued throughout the day. On a second trip to the grocery store, she lost her driver's license. God directed me to pray with her again on the phone. As I closed our prayer, I heard in my spirit, *She will find it—it's misplaced in her wallet.* As I started to tell her to check her wallet again, her cell phone dropped my call.

In the meantime, she headed to the parking lot, thinking she may have left her license in the car. There on the ground, by her car, was someone's paycheck in the amount of $800.

To the owner's delight, she was able to return it to them while they were still in the store. And to her delight, within the hour, she found her driver's license—in the wrong pocket of her wallet.

When she finally did get back to her kitchen, she called again. This time there was a problem with the cornstarch. It was past the expiration date. I paused to ask God for the right advice and heard, *Tell her to call her neighbor.*

Christy called her neighbor, Kristin, who had no cornstarch but cheerfully volunteered to go to the store and buy some. When Kristin dropped off the cornstarch, she offered to stay and help cook the meal. My daughter took her up on the kind offer and they cooked until 2:00 in the morning.

The day of our event finally dawned. The chicken was cooked and the birthday cake for Jesus was finished. I had used nine cake mixes, 27 eggs, six pounds of sugar and two and a half pounds of butter. Now, with the time for loading the car upon me, I realized the birthday cake for Jesus, resting on plywood, was too heavy for me to pick up! What was I going to do? I had to be on time. Not only did I have the dessert, I was the speaker!

As I stood frozen in the middle of the kitchen, the phone rang. It was a family friend who helped with yard work at the house. He said, "Hi Marty, I was calling to see if you needed me to help put any food in the car, since I figured you were getting ready to leave."

Stunned, but smiling, I said, "As a matter of fact—I do!"

The event began on time. Our guests raved that the food was better than ever and when the attendance was taken, there were exactly 125 ladies in attendance to carry all 125 gift baskets home.

Six more, equally amazing, events took place that day but I think you get the picture: God's power surrounds the details of His plan.

"And God is able to make all grace (every favor and earthly blessing) come to you in abundance, so that you may…require no aid or support…for every good work and charitable donation."

II CORINTHIANS 9:8 (AMP)

No amount of personality, talent, strength, intellect or money can secure the success and fulfillment that God's plan and enabling provide. The key to experiencing God's stabilizing power in your life, is getting in step with His plan—by acknowledging Him; seeking Him, in all the ways of your day!

The Lord will work out His plans for my life.

PSALM 138:8

CHAPTER 11

Learning NOT to Lean

We have learned that the decisions we make every day are either directed by the voice of our own human understanding or by the voice of God's understanding. The voice of our own understanding speaks out of our own desires and limited knowledge. The voice of God's understanding speaks out of God's desires and His unlimited knowledge.

> ...the Creator of the ends of the Earth, neither faints nor is weary, His understanding is unsearchable.
>
> ISAIAH 40:28 (NKJV)

It is interesting to watch news commentators point fingers in their effort to explain the reason for the mounting chaos in America and the world. I'm not a politician, but I do know who's responsible for the problems we are facing today. And it all goes back to the temptation we're discussing; the temptation to go our own way, instead of God's way.

If you think about it, the problems we're all facing today exist because Lucifer made the decision to lean on his own understanding. He allowed his personal desires and limited knowledge to cause him to defy God. The result was the creation of sin. And sin was able to enter our world because Adam and Eve chose to do the same thing: Lean away from the desires of the God who loved them and lean, instead, on their own understanding—to go their own way.

Jonah did it when he reasoned that the only way to be safe from the wicked city of Nineveh was to get in a boat and head opposite of the direction God had given him. And, as a result of doing what seemed safe to him, the men he was traveling with physically picked him up in the middle of a storm and threw him overboard, into a churning black sea.

It is this continued rebellion against God, today, that causes parents and spouses to leave home; to lean on a plan created by their own desires and limited knowledge, for happiness. It's what causes children to lean away from their parents' wisdom and run for the illusions the world is offering.

Some of us are living with painful consequences today because we chose to lean on our own understanding instead of leaning on the understanding of God.

You can make many plans but the Lord's purpose will prevail.
PROVERBS 19:21 (NLT)

I remember a day, thirty-eight years ago, when I made a decision to go in a direction opposite of the one God had given me. That single decision created winds of adversity that drove me into a storm God never intended for me to face.

Consequently, today, I am no longer interested in leaning on my own understanding—even in the smallest details of life. In the darkness of my life's storm I have found the light of God's mercy and I'm determined to make it to His harbor, each day, by obeying Him in all things.

In the darkness of Jonah's storm, God gave him a merciful, second chance to obey. And when we repent of leaning on our own understanding, in any decision, God will give us a second chance. God will redeem our wrong decisions and the fearful consequences that go with them, if we simply step into the boat of His will. There we'll find exactly what we're looking for; the safety of a life that satisfies and a love that does not disappoint.

There's an old song that says, "There's no disappointment in Jesus, He's all that He's promised to be."[5] That is true. Jesus eagerly waits to embrace us with the love every heart longs for; to dance us through the darkness of every storm, by the light of His direction.

Although many people would say they have sensed this loving Presence of God, in their lifetime, many of these same people would also admit they have not known exactly how to interact with Him on a moment-by-moment basis.

I have learned and declare again that there is only one thing we have to do to enjoy *this kind* of a relationship with God. We need simply to acknowledge Him—seek to become aware of Him in all of our physical ways. When we do, Proverbs 3:6 declares He will show us what to do in the everyday events of life.

CHAPTER 12

A Physical Requirement for Hearing

When Jesus walked the Earth, He ministered to people's physical needs first. And since there is one physical requirement necessary for distinguishing God's voice, we need to stop and consider it.

Again, for clarity, you and I are spirit-beings as well as physical-beings. We have a soul and we live in a physical body. And few would argue that the physical bodies we live in have no affect on our relationship with God. If you have ever tried to pray when you were tired, you know it's true!

The physical requirement for hearing God's voice is *a healthy mind.* And a healthy brain facilitates a healthy mind. A healthy mind is necessary to hear God's voice because our brain is our body's physical point of contact with the supernatural realm of God's Spirit.

> *When wisdom enters your heart, and knowledge is pleasant*
> *to your soul, discretion will preserve you; understanding will*

keep you, ...So you may walk in the way of goodness, and
keep to the paths of righteousness.

PROVERBS 2:10, 11 & 20 (NKJV)

As the physical point of contact with the realm of God's Spirit, our brain is a physiological organ. That means it has two parts. It has a physical part and it has a logical—thinking part. Just like the other organs in our body, the physical part of our brain needs proper nutrition, rest and exercise. In case you're wondering, we exercise our brain by studying and memorizing information. Take it from a grandmother: age-related memory loss is real. Our need for exercising our brain increases as we age. Memorizing Scripture is a good form of exercise for both parts of our brain. It strengthens our brain's capabilities physically, while it infuses truth in the thinking part of our brain.

My son, give attention to my words...For they are life to those
who find them, and health to all their flesh.

PROVERBS 4:20 & 22 (NKJV)

The Bible Cure for Memory Loss is a small book written by Dr. Don Colbert.[6] The easy reading it contains is filled with corrective and preventative measures for establishing a healthy mind. From it, I have learned that there are 50 neurotransmitters released in our brain as we are thinking. These neurotransmitters facilitate our ability to make decisions. And they are literally generated and affected by what we eat.

When we experience high levels of stress, as a result of being very troubled or even very excited, our bodies can burn these neurotransmitters up faster than our body can replace them. And when the body cannot keep up with the production of these necessary neurotransmitters, we can experience clinical depression.

Very simply, depression is caused by conflict. We experience conflict when our circumstances cause us to believe we will never have something we want or never get rid of something we don't want. A problem with depression is the body's way of telling our mind that positive change needs to take place in either our thinking or in our circumstances.

Depending on the severity of our need, doctors may temporarily prescribe synthetic neurotransmitters called antidepressants, until our mind is functioning normally—producing its own neurotransmitters again. When the physical function of our brain breaks down it is certainly no more wrong to take antidepressants than it would be to put our arm in a cast if a bone was broken.

The physical part of depression can be solved with medical intervention, nutrition, and rest. To solve the logical-thinking part of our depression we must, first, identify the conflict. We must identify exactly what it is we think we need to be happy or what it is we think we have to get rid of to be happy. Once the conflict is identified, we must then apply Biblical truth to our circumstances and trust God to provide relief and resolution, as we listen for His direction.

The problem of depression also opens a door for the problem of fear. In particular, because a woman's greatest need is security, her greatest enemy, by default, is fear. On a cautionary note, as we talk about being able to identify the voices that are speaking to us, man or woman, it is important to acknowledge that Satan and his demons are always looking for an opportunity to influence our behavior through the voice of our own human understanding. The latest Gallup poll indicates that 42% of Americans do believe people can be possessed by the devil.[7]

The Spirit clearly says that in later times some will abandon the faith and follow deceiving spirits and things taught by demons.
I TIMOTHY 4:1 (NIV)

Events that have occurred in our past can create a stronghold of fear in our life. If you struggle with irrational thoughts and voices—if you are tormented by "what ifs" that rob you of peace in daily living—restricting your ability to interact productively with others, I urge you to seek out solid Biblical teaching for dismantling those strongholds. Additionally, do seek prayer from those in your Biblical chain of authority.

Those troubled by evil spirits were cured...because power was coming from Him and healing them all.

LUKE 6:18 & 19 (NIV)

One day we will be set free from our mortal bodies and the difficulties they create for us physically and spiritually. But until God exchanges our mortal body for an immortal one, we must be prepared for the enemy's assault through the door of our own flesh.

Just as proper nutrition and rest are necessary for the physical part of our brain, sound biblical Truth is necessary for the thinking part of our brain. A lack of either one prohibits us from being able to process information correctly and prohibits us from having a healthy mind that can clearly distinguish God's voice.

CHAPTER 13

God In the Details You Betcha!

As you're reading through this book, don't allow your flesh to convince you that the events of daily living are unimportant to God. Scripture reveals that no incident is too small to receive His attention and direction. The tenth chapter of Matthew tells us that God sees every small, brown sparrow that falls to the ground and that He numbers the very hairs of our head.

The Bible is full of examples of God's direction in every-day events to accomplish divine purposes. He directed a Hebrew Mother to make a basket out of reeds, knowing it would be used to save the leader of His people. He directed a Father to send his youngest son to carry lunch to his brothers, knowing that before that boy returned home, he would have picked up his slingshot and killed the enemy of God's people. He directed a Hebrew couple to move, in the middle of the night, to save the newborn Savior of us all.

God desires to provide detailed direction in the daily events of life, for two reasons. First, He desires to build within us an unshakeable confidence in His direction. As I see the wonderful results of following God's direction in the *small* details of life, I'm compelled to release more complete control to Him in the *great* decisions of life.

Second, He provides detailed direction because we have been redeemed to accomplish His purposes in this world and not our own.

...for everything serves your plans.

PSALM 119:91

We exist to give God's desires expression on Earth. If I am not willing to give God the freedom to direct the details of my daily behavior, at what point *will* my life give His life expression?

Three things have happened as I have obeyed the detailed direction of God's voice over the years. First, life has taken on incredible order. And that order is facilitating a level of productivity I did not experience before. In turn, the spiritual and tangible blessing of God, to others, through me, has increased. When we listen to God, we are abiding in Him; the true vine. And the result is:

"By this My Father is glorified that you bear much fruit."

JOHN 15:8 (NKJV)

And, finally, an unshakable faith has taken over my heart. It is hard to doubt that God will provide for my life's greatest needs when I see Him demonstrate such great concern for the small ones.

I know what life looks like when I'm in control and I'm no longer interested in being in charge. Once you clear the hurdle of wanting to control your own life and decide to run God's race—letting Him determine what you do and when and where you do it—the adventure is addictive.

As your plan unfolds, even the simple can understand it. No wonder I wait expectantly for each of your commands.

PSALM 119:130-131

The supernatural power—the grace of God—does surround His plan. As we have discussed, the prize we are pursuing in listening for God's voice is the unshakable faith that results from a love relationship with Him. However, along the way, you and I will encounter plenty of evidence of God's existence. There is no earthly explanation for the phenomenal things that happen when you obey His voice!

> *I told you my plans and you replied. Now give me your instructions. Make me understand what you want; for then I shall see your miracles.*
>
> PSALM 119:26-27

Four Reasons God Speaks

I have said that God wants to speak to each of us for the same reason any other person wants to speak with the one they are in love with: Love, by its nature, desires intimate communication about anything and everything. Specifically, God's love compels Him to speak to us for these four reasons: to direct us, to protect us, to encourage us and to bless us.

For Direction

With regard to speaking to *direct* us, God has 5 objectives: **First, God speaks to direct us TO His specific plan.** I have said that the needs of this world are too great for God to send us wandering through a day, relying on circumstances alone to reveal what He wants us to do. David said:

> *Tell me what to do, Oh Lord and make it plain.*
>
> PSALM 27:11

God has detailed plans to care for our needs so that we can reproduce spiritual life in others. And He intends that we be able to identify those plans in the daily events of life.

I heard the phrase, "walk in the Spirit" many times growing up, but no one ever explained exactly how to do it. For that reason, I assumed it was a general spiritual phrase that meant I was supposed to try hard not to sin and confess it quickly when I did.

The Spirit of God has since helped me understand that we "walk in the Spirit" when we walk out God's desires or "will" as He reveals it to us through His written Word or by His Voice. When we identify what it is God wants us to do and do it, we are walking out behavior generated by the desires of God. We are "Walking in the Spirit".

...those who follow after the Holy Spirit find themselves doing those things that please God.

ROMANS 8:5

There is no thrill that compares to identifying and obeying God's direction; doing exactly what Jesus would do if He was on Earth and could do, Himself, what He's just asked of you! God's voice directs us TO His plan for us.

Secondly, God's voice directs us to the human resources for His plan. When we think of resources, we usually think of money or tangible objects. One quick illustration of God's voice directing me to resources, again, involves buying gifts.

One day my sister called to tell me a local store had small pumpkins on sale for fifty cents. She thought I might like to include them in the Thanksgiving baskets we would be passing out. I hadn't thought of that. I agreed they'd be a colorful addition and thanked her for the suggestion. Since we were still two weeks out from the meeting, I decided to wait a few days before making a trip to the store.

Finally, one morning, early in the week of the event, I decided I would have my devotions and then head out to buy pumpkins. Over and over again, as I tried to concentrate on the Scripture I was reading, I kept hearing, *Call Rhonda, at work*. Rhonda was a friend who co-founded JFWC with me. I tried to ignore what I was hearing, reasoning that since my friend was at work, she shouldn't be bothered. When it finally occurred to me that this persistent voice was God's voice, I picked up the phone and called her number.

Just before we closed our short conversation, she said, "By the way, I keep forgetting to tell you, one of the ladies who attends JFWC wants to donate several baskets of small pumpkins and gourds to us, to use however we want."

Needless to say, I didn't go shopping after my devotions. God thought pumpkins were a good idea too and paid the bill Himself. God's voice speaks to direct us to the resources for His plan.

Tangible items are certainly not the only resource we need to fulfill God's plans. And, thankfully, Philippians 4:19 (NKJV) says:

And my God shall supply all your need according to His riches in glory by Christ Jesus.

If you are as busy as I am, you know that resources of time and energy are as crucial to God's plans as money and tangible items are. We may know that God wants us to do something nice for someone, but many times we neglect to act because we don't know where we'll get the time or energy.

As I have obeyed God's detailed leading throughout the years, I have watched Him multiply my limited time and energy as miraculously as He multiplied the five small loaves and two little fish that fed those 5,000 hungry men and all of their families. As Proverbs 10:27 states:

Reverence for God adds hours to each day.

God extends our time, sustains our energy, and stretches our dollars to meet our needs and bless the lives of others. Another old song says, "Little is much, when God is in it."[8]

A story that illustrates this wonderful truth also took place while I was shopping for the gifts we give out at JFWC. Whether you're a grandparent or not, you know energy can definitely be a limited resource. And, on this day, I was running out of it as I walked the aisles of a very large warehouse. As you've already read, I typically purchased a lot of items at once to save money. For that reason, it certainly wasn't unusual for me to be on my feet for three or four hours at a time.

I was halfway finished with my shopping when I remembered the warehouse I was in had vending machines. Instantly feeling better, I thought about the energy boost I'd get from a can of pop and a package of cheese crackers. With that thought, I took off for the machines.

I was speeding down the aisle, trying not to run anyone over when I suddenly heard a taunting voice say, *You probably don't have any change.*

Abruptly, I stopped my cart. I had no idea whether or not I had any change. Fumbling through my purse, I grabbed my wallet and yanked back the zipper on my change purse. My heart sank. I had exactly one dollar in change.

Vending machines were a familiar business to me. Over the years, I had been responsible for keeping the machines at my husband's office building filled with snacks. I sadly reasoned my dollar wouldn't even buy the pop.

As I heaved my loaded cart around, I heard these two simple words, **Check anyway.** Heaving my cart back in the direction of the machines, I rolled on over. And, to my thirsty surprise, their cans of pop were less than a dollar. They were sixty-five cents!

I quickly made my thirsty selection and then shot a stray glance toward the snack machines. Surely I couldn't afford anything else, but what could it hurt to read along the price bar?

Sauntering over to the machines, I sipped my pop, while I read along the price bar. All of a sudden, I said, out loud, "Are you serious?"

They actually did have one item for thirty-five cents. And yes in-deed, I looked up to see that it was, in fact, my cheese crackers! I'm sure the people around me wondered why the lady with the packed cart, kept saying, "Thank you, God," out loud. With one dollar, God supplied my heart's specific desire and restored my energy, enabling me to accomplish His plan for my day.

Third, God's voice directs us to the spiritual power for His plan. Power over sin increases as we acknowledge that God is speaking to us. As I began to recognize that God was speaking to me, I discovered that I had increased power to obey Him and I wondered, why?

Certainly, when we recognize that *it is God* telling us what to do we should have greater motivation to obey. I remember that my children had increased power to obey authority when I headed for the plastic spoon in our kitchen drawer. But power to obey God doesn't increase because of the fear of being punished by Him. If we're honest, many of us have pushed right through the fear of being punished to do a variety of things we knew we'd pay for. Identifying God's voice increases our power to obey by providing us with the opportunity to do what we talked about earlier—to walk in the Spirit.

Walk in the Spirit and you shall not fulfill the lusts of the flesh.
GALATIANS 5:16 (NKJV)

It is possible to live above patterns of sin we have struggled with our whole life by walking in the Spirit—identifying and obeying God's specific direction. Walking in the spirit increases our power to obey two ways.

The first one, we have mentioned. When we recognize God is speaking to us, we have pinpointed His plan. And when we obey it, we step into the all-sufficient power that surrounds it.

And secondly, as we step into that power, the power permeates us.

...Christ's mighty energy is at work within me.
COLOSSIANS 1:29

Jesus conquered the power of sin. He never submitted to it the entire time He lived on Earth. And in so doing, He paved a sin-free path, for us, on this sin-dominated Earth. The voice of His Spirit's direction, leads us along that very paved, righteous path of obedience, Jesus forged. On it, we receive all the faith, will, strength and right attitude necessary to accomplish God's plan. Therefore, as we obey what we "hear"—we do not sin.

And you know…that there is no sin in Him, no missing of God's will at any time in any way. So if we stay close to Him, we won't be sinning either.

I JOHN 3:5 & 6

Fourth, God's voice directs us to the ultimate purpose of His plans; Christ-likeness for us and for others. As we have learned, God is in the business of conforming us to the exact likeness of His own Son. Again, as our teacher, the Holy Spirit has one goal woven through all of the daily direction He gives us—to reproduce Jesus in us. I Corinthians 15:49 tells us that just as we have borne the image of the man of dust, one day we will bear the image of the heavenly Man.

But we all…are being transformed into the same image from glory to glory, just as by the Spirit of the Lord.

II CORINTHIANS 3:18 (NKJV)

And as Jesus becomes visible in us, God intends that we reveal Him to those who don't know Him. He wants to use what He is forging in us, to reproduce spiritual life in others. When we Walk in the Spirit, following God's voice of direction, we allow God to make a path with our life, where the Son of God can be seen. The Apostle Paul said:

Brethren, join in following my example, and note those who
so walk, as you have us for a pattern.

PHILIPPIANS 3:17 (NKJV)

God puts Himself on display in us to provide strength for
those who already know Him and salvation for those who do not.
God directs some of us to plant seeds and others to harvest the
fruit that comes from those seeds.

The one who plants and the one who waters work together
with the same purpose. And both will be rewarded for their
own hard work.

I CORINTHIANS 3:8 (NLT)

Fifth, God's voice directs us to the eternal rewards that
accompany His various plans. The Bible says that when we
stand before God in Heaven, at the Judgment Seat of Christ, the
glorious light of His Presence is going to cause our collection of
works on Earth, laying before Him, to burst into flame. When
the fire is finished burning, the only accomplishments left will
be those we carried out as a result of *obedience to the Holy Spirit's*
direction. For those accomplishments, only, we will be rewarded
(I Corinthians 3:13-14).

It's important to stop and think about that. We can try to gain
God's approval by performing good deeds of our own choosing. But
it's the *particular deeds of God's own will* that are important to Him.
For this reason, it is impossible to underestimate the importance of
knowing how to identify God's direction in our daily living. God
in the details? You Betcha!

CHAPTER 14

Protection, Encouragement and Blessing

J ehovah Himself is caring for you! He is your defender. He protects
you day and night. He keeps you from all evil, and preserves your
life. He keeps His eye upon you as you come and go, and always
guards you.

PSALM 121:5-8

Not only does God speak to direct us, God speaks to protect us.

For Protection

Hearing and obeying God's voice provides physical and spiritual
protection. Each of us can tell our own stories about God's physical
protection over the course of our lives; like the times we have heard
the repeated directive to pull off at a rest stop on the highway.
Perhaps you can even remember hearing, *"Wake up"* just before
nodding off behind the wheel.

At the same time, many of us know of Christians who have
gone on to Heaven by accidental means that we still struggle to
understand. We must never lose sight of the truth that it is God

who appoints our purpose and God who ordains when that purpose is fulfilled. Until that moment comes, God's voice of direction will provide physical protection for the lives of His children on Earth.

Not only does God speak to protect us physically, He speaks to protect us spiritually. Speaking of the Holy Spirit, Jesus said:

> *"He will guide you into all truth..."*
>
> JOHN 16:13 (NKJV)

Many people claim to speak for God. Therefore we must always remember to lay what we hear about God against the truth of His written Word. God's voice speaks to protect us from believing teaching that violates truth.

> *And the Spirit is the one who testifies, because the Spirit is the truth.*
>
> I JOHN 5:6 (NIV)

Further, God's voice protects us spiritually by convicting us of sin. The voice of the Holy Spirit is a warning system to protect us from the danger of sin's destructive consequences. Again, speaking of the Holy Spirit, Jesus said:

> *"And when He has come, He will convict the world of sin, and of righteousness and of judgment."*
>
> JOHN 16:8 (NKJV)

Speaking of Himself, Jesus said:

> *"...if you follow me, you won't be stumbling through the darkness, for living light will flood your path."*
>
> JOHN 8:12

For Encouragement

Not only does God speak to direct us and protect us, God speaks to encourage us in our walk of faith. There are times when God encourages me with sweet words and personal promises. Other times, His voice orchestrates circumstances to encourage me.

One particular day, the weight of my circumstances and responsibilities was clearly getting the best of me. It's safe to say I was deeply discouraged. I looked over the long list of errands I had to run and knew I'd have to push to leave the house if I was going to successfully whittle the list down.

I picked up my keys to leave, several times, only to be held back by one phone call after another. The interruptions were so strategic, that I finally said out loud, "God it's quite obvious, you're not ready for me to leave yet!"

Eventually the calls did stop. And in the quiet, I heard four simple words, *Now you can go.*

More than happy to obey, I pulled out of my driveway and headed south, down the main road nearest my home. This typically busy road was oddly solitary for early afternoon. Nonetheless, it was flooded with comforting sunshine that beckoned me on. I was happy to finally be on my way.

Suddenly, out of nowhere—right in front of me—the shadow of large wings appeared on the road. Larger by far than any I had ever seen, honest-to-goodness wings were flying directly ahead of my car. Staring in disbelief, I strained repeatedly at the side window; pressing my cheek against the cold glass to catch a glimpse of the creature flying above me. I realized it had to be a bird of some kind. But it was no use; regardless of what it was—I was only going to be able to see its shadow.

The bird continued flying with great strength and purpose, as if it had been assigned to lead me. When the road curved left, the wings cut left. When the road curved right, the wings cut right. For several solemn minutes, I watched in wonder as the shadow of those graceful wings stayed right with my car.

Then, as suddenly as they appeared—they disappeared. And when they did I woke from my sweet stupor to find those wings had carried my discouragement away with them. In His wonder-filled way God had just let me know—by winged messenger—that He was right with me. His grace was more than sufficient for all I was facing.

...hide me in the shadow of your wings as you hover over me.
PSALM 17:8

There is only one person who knows exactly how we feel. God alone can speak the encouraging words and orchestrate the circumstances to calm our fears and bid our sorrows cease.

Blessed be the God and Father of our Lord Jesus Christ, the Father of mercies and God of all comfort, who comforts us in all our affliction, so that we may be able to comfort those who are in any affliction, with the comfort with which we ourselves are comforted by God.
II CORINTHIANS 1:3-4 (ESV)

For Blessing

Finally, God speaks to bless us. To our delight, we have learned that when our life is surrendered to God's plans we experience supernatural power in daily living. Again that is true because God's power surrounds His plans for us—not our plans for ourselves.

Speaking of being blessed, in case I haven't mentioned it yet, I have been blessed with eight wonderful grandchildren. And yes, if you'd like to come over, I have plenty of pictures to show you.

Fortunately for them, my "love language" happens to be "gift giving". How I love watching their faces as they tear into surprises I've picked out just for them. Whether the gift is large or small, they are always excited to receive it. Their delight is one of my highest pleasures.

As you might imagine, many of the details of my daily living involve buying gifts. And as I follow God's plan for my day, I am always astounded by the way He helps me with my shopping.

Each Christmas I have a particular theme for the gifts I buy my grandchildren. A recent Christmas theme was the "Chronicles of Narnia". They love the story. I bought the boys a knight's costume, Abby, a princess costume and completed all their ensembles with rubber swords (which, I might add, was a wise move on my part). Finally, I planned to top the theme off by ordering each of them a stuffed toy version of the various animals that were featured in the Narnia story. At the time, I had five grandchildren so I needed five animals.

I ordered a large lion with a sweet face to represent Aslan for my granddaughter Abby, a large colorful cheetah for my wild animal lover Caleb and two soft beavers for my youngest grandsons, Gabriel and Chase. All I needed to be finished with my shopping was one life-like fox for my 5-year-old grandson, Charlie.

After some browsing, I located the particular fox I wanted at an online toy company. I printed off the phone number and item number and laid the paper aside. Days later, when I reached the company by phone, I was regretfully informed the item I wanted was out of stock. However, they did say they were hopeful they would receive another shipment before Christmas.

The following week, I called back multiple times. When an actual sales person finally answered, I was told the stuffed animals came from overseas in large crates. They explained that they were never sure which animals they would receive. I was invited to call back as often as I liked.

Shortly after Thanksgiving, I was sitting at my desk completely absorbed with some writing I needed to finish, when I noticed the paper I had printed off from the toy company. It was laying on the right side of my desk. As I glanced over at the paper, I simply heard, *Call now*. Hopeful that God was up to something good, I picked up the phone and dialed the number.

A kind lady on the other end of the line told me that the warehouse had just received a large shipment of various stuffed animals. When I asked her if they had received a red fox, she explained that looking for any kind of fox would be like looking for a needle in a haystack.

When I politely explained why the fox was so important to me, she asked if I had the specific item number for the one I wanted. Glancing down at the paper in my hand, I quickly gave her the number. She asked me to hold on while she tried to locate someone in the warehouse and warned me it could take a while. I gratefully told her I was more than happy to wait. Within a matter of seconds she came back on the line and said in a very excited voice, "Mrs. Carroll, the very one you want is sitting right here by my desk. Now that's a miracle."

Nice story, Marty. But sometimes things just 'work out' for people— whether they're Christians or not.

That's absolutely true. But also true is the reality that things work out for me with amazing regularity! And why would God help me or any of us this way? Again, first and most importantly, God uses these small events to establish faith in His direction so that we will not waver in following Him as He leads us to accomplish His greatest purposes for our life.

Secondly, God has promised to provide both the material and spiritual resources for His will. Quite apparently, God wanted my grandson to have the red fox; He must love the Narnia story too.

And all these blessings shall come upon you and overtake you, because you obey the voice of the Lord your God...
DEUTERONOMY 28:2 (NKJV)

Then, finally, God is a man of His word.

"But seek ye first the kingdom of God, and his righteousness; and all these things shall be added unto you."
MATTHEW 6:33 (KJV)

God delights to grant the specific desires of our heart that are in keeping with His will. God wants to communicate with us regarding the details of life. We are in the process of learning how to identify God's voice so He can direct us, protect us, encourage us and bless us.

CHAPTER 15

What Does God's Voice Sound Like?

Sweet by Any Name

We have learned that God has made provision for directing the activity of our lives five different ways, apart from the conscious awareness of His voice. One of the ways He directs us is through the witness of the Holy Spirit. Again, the witness of the Holy Spirit is our God-given ability to distinguish God's very Presence and will. God speaks out of this witness of His Spirit.

If you have been a Christian for very long, I'm sure you can think of times when God has influenced you to do something particular for someone else. After obeying this sense of what God wanted you to do, have you ever tried to explain to others how you knew to do it? I have heard people describe direction from God these various ways:

(1) I felt like it was the "right thing" to do.

(2) I was "impressed" to do it.

(3) I had an "impulse" and I followed through with it.

(4) It seemed like a "good idea".

(5) The "thought" just came to me.

(6) I felt "compelled" to do it.

(7) God "led" me to do it.

These various descriptions describe the direction I am explaining to be God's voice.

In the book, *The Hole In Our Gospel*, Richard Stern, CEO of World Vision, quotes a prominent businessman. The gentleman he quotes played a vital role in getting him to take the top leadership position for the ministry.

Mr. Stern's friend strongly urged him to interview for the job, saying, "Don't ask me to explain it but God told me you are going to be the next President of World Vision."[9]

Mr. Stern did become the CEO of World Vision and although his friend was not asked to explain how God spoke to him, revealing what was to come, God *has* directed me to explain it; to explain the process of how God communicates with us so that His specific desires can be "walked-out" on the Earth.

Inside Ears

I want to begin my explanation by saying that without a doubt, everyone's first question regarding hearing God's voice, is, "What does it sound like?"

We know from the Old Testament that when God spoke to the children of Israel, God's voice thundered from a mountain so powerfully the people covered their ears and begged for Him to stop speaking. Today, God does not speak loudly from the top of a mountain. Today, He speaks from within our mortal bodies.

Here's a quick exercise that is very effective in helping you hear what God's voice sounds like.

Please answer the following questions silently, to yourself.

Where were you when you prayed to trust Jesus as your Savior? (Don't say it out loud!)

How many years have you been a Christian?

Silently, to yourself, sing the first line of the hymn, "Amazing Grace".

The audible nature of God's voice sounds like the voice you just heard answering those questions. In the event you're thinking, *What I just heard sounds like my voice*, that's true. And it's true because God speaks through the microphone of our spirit. For that reason, what we hear, in large part, sounds like our voice. Nonetheless, this is what Scripture says about the Holy Spirit speaking through human vessels:

"...do not worry beforehand about what to say. Just say whatever is given you at the time, for it is not you speaking, but the Holy Spirit."

MARK 13:11 (NIV)

As this short exercise demonstrates we do actually *hear* our thoughts inwardly, just as we hear sounds outwardly. When you silently sang the first line of "Amazing Grace", you did not hear the words as a monotone cadence. You heard the words as a melody. We have ears on the inside that enable us to hear and therefore respond to what is going on within us, just as we have ears on the outside that enable us to hear and respond to what is going on around us.

Eight times in the New Testament Jesus refers to the "ears of our understanding", when He says:

"He that has ears to hear, let him hear."

MATTHEW 11:15 (NKJV)

Over and over again in Scripture, Jesus links receiving spiritual direction with "hearing". In Isaiah 50:4 (AMP) the prophet said,

He wakens my ear to hear as a disciple (as one who is taught).

In John 10:27 (NKJV), Jesus said:

"My sheep hear my voice; and I know them, and they follow me."

In John 18:37 (NKJV), He said:

"Everyone who is of the truth hears my voice."

God *does* speak today. His voice is small, soft and still. During this church age, He intends that we be the ones who do the shouting from high places.

"...what you hear whispered in your ear; proclaim upon the housetops."

MATTHEW 10:27 (NAS)

God speaks softly, in our mind, with thoughts we can hear. By the way—the word picture for the Greek translation of the word "comfort" (used in Philippians 2:1) portrays the Lord coming close and whispering words of gentle cheer or tender counsel in a believer's ear.

This opportunity to hear God speak is a privilege I cannot fully comprehend. It is humbling that we carry the treasure of His voice in the earthen vessel of our physical body.

On the unfortunate side of that wonder is this reality: Because we live in a body subject to sin, our reception is not always clear. We have said that the mind of flesh makes decisions out of its own desires and limited knowledge. And because it does, it will never make it easy for us to yield control to God. Our flesh works to create interference. Consider what Paul said:

*For I know that nothing good dwells in me, that is, in my
flesh…I see a different law in the members of my body,
waging war against the law of my mind…*

ROMANS 7:18 & 23 (AMP)

Again, Proverbs 3 speaks of only two voices seeking to guide
Christians in making daily decisions: the voice of the Holy Spirit—
the voice that communicates *God's desires* to us, (referred to as
the Mind of Christ, in I Corinthians 2:16) and the voice of our
own human understanding; the voice that communicates *its own
desires* to us, (referred to as the Mind of the Flesh, in Romans 8:6).
Importantly, the Mind of the Flesh is also the party line Satan uses
to communicate with us. *All the material going forward is dedicated
to helping you distinguish the difference between the two.*

A Day at the Divine Chalkboard

When I was a young mother of 23, God began teaching me how
to hear His voice with an exercise of His own. One sunny day in
May, I was carrying a basket loaded with folded clothes back and
forth from the laundry room to the bedrooms. On my first trip to
the bedrooms, I noticed the glass vase of flowers a neighbor had
given me sitting on the television. Now that several days had passed,
the flowers were dropping petals and the water had turned brown.
They no longer smelled sweet!

As I approached the flowers, I clearly heard the thought, *Pour
the water out of the vase and throw the flowers away.*

So I did what some of you may have done. I completely disregarded what I heard. I walked right by the flowers, unloaded my
basket, and headed back to the laundry room.

Three times I walked past those flowers. And each time I heard
the same thing. *Pour the water out of the vase and throw the
flowers away.*

On my last necessary pass, the voice of God's Spirit was so emphatic it stopped me completely in my tracks. And in a matter of only moments, the witness of the Holy Spirit helped me understand that it was God who was drawing my attention to this vase of flowers.

Completely captivated, I set my laundry basket down and sat on the couch beside the flowers. As I sat still, God brought this verse to mind:

> *We destroy arguments…raised against the knowledge of God, and take every thought captive to obey Christ.*
>
> II CORINTHIANS 10:5 (ESV)

I listened to the words of that verse as I repeated them over and over again in my mind. Suddenly, I said out loud, "I get it!" God is teaching me to capture a particular thought and consider its source. In this particular case, God was speaking to my procrastinating flesh; directing me to do with the flowers what was undeniably necessary.

The more I thought about what had just happened, the more excited I got. I wondered what the results would be if I applied what I had just learned to *everything I heard in my head* going forward. What if I stopped and paid attention to these audible thoughts that were persistently directing me to take some action, and then obeyed them?

It sounded like an interesting game. So—for the day—I decided to play. I said, "Okay, Lord, today I'm going to seek to do what II Corinthians 10:5 says. I'm going to capture the persistent thoughts I hear and ask the question, 'Where did this thought come from?' If the result of doing what I hear is a good thing— I'm going to assume You are the One behind it!"

My first move was to get rid of the flowers. I poured out the water and put the vase away. Throughout the rest of the day, I listened for these same persistent thoughts. Some of them were as simple as, *Put your shoes away*, or *Put the clothes in the dryer*.

As the days went by, God's Spirit carefully taught me how to identify which internally audible thoughts were coming from Him.

As I identified these thoughts and successively obeyed the directives I heard, this is what I found: My laundry got done every day because my children took better naps. In spite of all the activity associated with these three small children, my housework got done; our home was spotless and orderly. And last, but not least, I served a full meal each night, complete with dessert, on time.

There was so much order in my new life, I had the courage to start a women's Bible study for my friends and their friends. And each time they rang the doorbell I was amazed. Not only was my house clean, I was clean and well prepared; both with something delicious from my kitchen and with something eternally nutritious from God's Word.

Further, in addition to all this new order, my checkbook got fatter! The voice of God's Spirit directed me to bargains that saved more money than my coupon clipping did. I can remember shaking my head and wondering out loud, "What has changed in my home?" Thought by conscious thought, God gave me the opportunity to experience the order that exists when He is given the opportunity to direct the day's activity.

CHAPTER 16

That's Impossible!

Some people have responded with frustration to this teaching; that God wants us to take audible thoughts captive and make them obedient to Christ. They say, "That's impossible. Thousands of thoughts fleet through our mind. How can we possibly grab every one and ask, 'Where did this thought come from?'"

What about that question? Out of all the thoughts we have, which thoughts are we to capture and consider? We do have countless thoughts bombarding our minds at any given time.

As a result of my own lessons at the chalkboard I can tell you two clear categories of thoughts God would not expect us to capture and consider. The first category of thoughts would be reflexive thoughts that sustain our physical life; unconscious thoughts like pick-up your feet and walk or pick-up your fork and eat. Secondly, God does not intend that we capture the thoughts that catalogue the factual information we have retained throughout our *lifetime*; the thoughts we recall when we need to use the knowledge we have. We don't need to capture and carefully consider the thought that one and one add up to two.

The thoughts God would have us capture and consider are those that *prompt us to take action in what we think, do and say.* If an audible thought prompts us to take righteous action in what we think, do or say—if it prompts us to do something Jesus would do—it is to our great benefit to obey what we've heard. By doing so, we will be blessed and others will be blessed as we give God's will expression on Earth.

If, after capturing an audible thought, we understand it is prompting us to take some sinful action, we are to reject it. Obviously if we do, we'll bypass the painful consequence the action carries with it. If we want to live a righteous life—a holy life—we must know when our flesh's appetite for sin is prompting our behavior.

It is critical that we listen to what we are "hearing" on the inside. It is critical because one of two powerful sources is speaking to direct our behavior!

It is not possible to consider every thought that our physical brains generate. But it *is* possible and *crucial* that we capture and consider the conscious, persistent, internally audible thoughts that prompt us to action; the thoughts we easily disregard, every day. It is crucial because some of them are coming from the *Throne of God* to direct us and bless us. It is crucial because others are coming from *spirits of darkness* and from the *darkness of our own flesh*— to stop God's blessing and bring destruction.

God's plans have detail just as ours do. And we will see that no thought is too small to be significant. Again, the thoughts God wants us to capture and consider are specifically those thoughts that *prompt us to action in what we think, do and say.*

The Gift of Choice

At this point, it is important to clarify that, as human beings fearfully and wonderfully made by God, we have been infused with the gift of choice. And God intends that we exercise that choice responsibly to sustain our mortal life and honor Him. Therefore, God does not dictate all of our behavior. Many times I have asked for God's direction regarding details that seemed important to me only to hear Him say I was free to choose.

In other words, not all choices made out of the desires of our own human understanding—our own flesh—are wrong. As moral agents, God intends that we enjoy making many of the necessary choices in life on our own.

Specifically, although our thoughts come from only two sources (the Mind of Christ and the Mind of the Flesh) there are two modes under which the Mind of our Flesh can operate. It can operate *inside* the framework of God's truth with behavior that's acceptable to God, or *outside* the framework of God's truth with behavior that's unacceptable to God.

As we exercise our choice, we must remember two things. First, as we make personal choices, we must remain aware that at any time the carnal power of our flesh's thinking can switch modes and run us in a direction that is clearly opposite of God's revealed will. In other words, with our choice we can sin in a hurry!

Secondly, we must remember that a matter of choice we have engaged in before can change to become a sinful choice when God clearly reveals He wants us to do something different.

To help illustrate the difference between all three options: (1) being directed by the Mind of Christ (God's voice), (2) being directed by the Mind of the Flesh operating *inside* the framework of God's truth and (3) being directed by the Mind of the Flesh operating *outside* the framework of God's truth, I'll use a personal illustration.

One New Year's Day, my youngest son and his wife were packing up their Christmas presents to head back to their home in Virginia. Over the years that my son attended college there, I always packed a lunch for his trip back and topped it with some cash for his gas tank.

Jordan and Micah were outside packing the car as I stood in the kitchen, when I heard the thought, *Their finances are tight, I should give them some gas money.* That thought came from the Mind of the Flesh—the voice of my own human understanding—operating *inside* the framework of God's truth. I know that after giving God His portion of my income, I am free to do whatever I want with the rest. Knowing it's better to give than receive, I exercised my choice and headed for my purse.

When I opened my wallet, I suddenly remembered that the only money I had was $150.00 in grocery money that I needed to stretch, for an indefinite period of time. Yet, from the voice of my own human understanding, I internally heard myself say, *I'll give them $50.00 of this money anyway. God will take care of me.*

As I reached for a $50.00 bill, suddenly I heard the Mind of Christ—God's voice—speak. In a clearly audible thought, I heard, **Give them $100.00.** At which time, needless to say, the Mind of the Flesh—the voice of my own understanding—abruptly switched modes. It threw a small fit that could definitely be classified as behavior operating outside of God's truth.

In high-pitched tones, internally, my flesh began listing sensible reasons for ignoring what God had just revealed He wanted me to do. Repeatedly, it insisted that I only give $50.00 away. While "it" was still objecting, I chose to overrule "it" and grabbed two $50.00 bills anyway. Once in hand, I hid them in my son's wallet.

Twenty minutes later, when I was sure they were safely way down the road, I sent Jordan and Micah a text to tell them about God's surprise. My son's protective side chided me at first, but as we closed our conversation, He gratefully thanked me for the gift.

For the next eight hours, I stayed busy with paperwork. Finally, around midnight, I climbed the stairs and headed for bed. When the time came to throw back the comforter and crawl in, I was shocked to find an envelope partially hidden under my pillow. More than curious, I quickly tore the envelope open. It was a card from my son and daughter-in-law thanking me for the meals and fun we enjoyed while we were together. And inside the card was a $50.00 bill.

God's voice of direction speaks out of His unlimited knowledge. The amount He directed me to give that afternoon, took into consideration His knowledge that $50.00 was hidden under my pillow!

We are free to follow our own human understanding, inside the framework of God's truth. But when God speaks to reveal His will to us, we must be ready to resist the reasoning voice of our flesh's wisdom. If not, we will miss the reward of God's purpose.

Again, our thoughts come from two sources: The Mind of our Flesh and the Mind of Christ. To be effective for the Kingdom, we have to be able to recognize the audible thoughts that are coming from the Spirit of God, within us. As we heed the voice of God's direction—walking out the behavior His Spoken and Written Word generate—the impossible becomes possible!

CHAPTER 17

Four Characteristics of His Voice

I have described what God's voice sounds like. And now that you know what to expect, let's explore a more expansive description of His wonderful voice.

[1] The voice of the Holy Spirit is soft. In I Kings 19:11 (AMP), Elijah encountered the Presence of God and heard Him speak. The Bible tells us that God's Presence was accompanied by a wind so strong it tore mountains into pieces. In the very next verse, verse 12, we read a description of the voice Elijah heard:

And after the earthquake a fire, but the Lord was not in the fire; and after the fire (a sound of gentle stillness and) a still, small voice.

Maybe you know someone who always speaks softly. If you do, you know that when they speak, you have to listen more carefully than you do when other people speak. The voice of the Holy Spirit is soft. And if we are going to hear Him, we must learn to listen carefully. The tone of His voice is still; it carries a calming sense of security.

[2] Although it is soft and still, Psalm 29:4 tells us: The voice of the Holy Spirit is powerful and full of majesty. A voice of authority does not have to speak loudly to elicit honor and convey power. My mother never raised her voice to me but I knew to listen when she spoke.

Unfortunately, on more than one occasion, my flesh has dared to question God. And may I say that when He has had to repeat His response, His powerful voice can resonate. I assure you, though it is still, God's voice can still be emphatic.

The voice of the Lord is powerful. The voice of the Lord is full of majesty.

PSALM 29:4 (NKJV)

The sound of the Holy Spirit's voice of direction is very different from the voice of the flesh's direction. The flesh's direction has a loud clamoring tone like that of a fast-talking salesman. It works to push you to action with a sense of pressure. "Get closer to the front of the line!" Don't let them take that away from you!" Why wait, you deserve it!" "Buy it now—buy it now!" The flesh's intention is to drown out the voice of God's Spirit within you. I don't know about you, but I've had to return my share of merchandise purchased as a result of impulse buying.

There is no clamoring sense of pressure when God speaks. He is not subject to time. He has all the power necessary to provide the resources for His plan. All He needs from us is submission.

[3] Although His voice is soft, the voice of the Holy Spirit is persistent. Speaking to His beloved Israel, God said:

Your ears shall hear a word behind you saying, "This is the way, walk in it," whenever you turn to the right hand or whenever you turn to the left.

ISAIAH 30:21 (NKJV)

The Hebrew word for "behind" is 'achar (akh-ar'). It means "to follow after". God's voice is soft but persistent. The voice of His direction follows after us, giving us ample opportunity to obey Him. His voice will repeatedly speak His will, the audible thought will not go away. He will only stop speaking when we willfully choose to disregard what He has said. Tragically, at that point, we will miss the benefit of His direction. For this reason, the blessing of God is tied to *immediate obedience*.

An example that demonstrates the merciful persistence of God's voice took place one June afternoon as my daughter and I were shopping for a suit for my son-in-law's birthday.

Curtis had taken the time to create a wish list online and had even posted a picture of the exact suit he wanted. Unfortunately, in my hurry to leave the house, I left without looking at it!

When we finally arrived at the mall, my daughter and I were both excited to find that one of our favorite stores had a long rack of men's suits on sale. Not wasting any time, we enthusiastically began looking through them—Christy on one side of the rack and me on the other. As I worked my way down my side, I repeatedly heard the word *"gray"*.

This would be a good place for me to say that we can miss the beneficial direction of God's voice for a variety of reasons. Strong emotion is one of those reasons. And on this day I was definitely experiencing strong emotion—the strong emotion of a woman in the height of a shopping mall frenzy. My giddiness definitely disrupted my ability to listen. Although I kept hearing the word gray, I ignored it—just like you ignore a child repeatedly tugging on your coattail.

I asked my daughter what color she thought her husband wanted most. She wasn't sure but casually suggested I buy a black one. Having confidence in her knowledge and taste, I selected a black suit in his size and hung it on my cart.

In spite of my decision, I continued hearing the word *"gray"*. I heard it so clearly I finally decided to mention it to my daughter. Somewhat apologetically, I explained that although I didn't want to ignore her advice I was continually hearing the word, *"gray"*. She laughed and said she wasn't going to compete with God and told me I was free to buy the gray suit if I wanted.

Hesitantly, I hung the black suit back on the rack and selected a gray one. I purchased it and, upon arriving home, wrapped it for the party. When the time came for opening presents, I nervously watched my son-in-law's face as he opened the box. He loved the suit. He tried it on and thanked me more than once for buying him such a nice gift. Best of all, the next day, he printed off his wish list to show me that I had indeed picked out the exact suit he wanted—light gray with a thin blue and yellow pin stripe. God's voice is soft but, thankfully, it's persistent!

[4] God's voice carries an inner assurance that erases anxiety.

"And when He brings out His own sheep, He goes before them; and the sheep follow Him, for they know his voice."
JOHN 10:4 (NKJV)

In anxious moments, the sound of God's voice will quiet anxiety and establish a sense of assurance in our heart. It is something you must experience to understand. No other voice can do that.

If you have children, maybe you can remember how you felt the first time they spent the night away from home or went out on a date. There was a tendency to be anxious as you waited for them to arrive back safely. On such occasions, over the years, I have mercifully been blessed to hear the words, *"They are safe. Everything is alright."*

How do I know its God speaking in those moments? I'm familiar with His voice. My physical fear dissipates just like mist in the sun. God's voice carries an assurance that quiets anxiety.

God may use a person to speak His peace to our heart. Perhaps you can remember when a parent or friend's voice has calmed your fears with an assurance you knew, came from beyond that person.

Regardless of the avenue God uses, once He speaks, we must choose to accept His assurance. The fear-provoking voice of our flesh will continually challenge what we've heard in order to keep us upset. Our flesh will always fight against our choice to listen to God and trust Him. God's soft, still voice is full of majesty and power. It's persistent and it quiets anxiety.

CHAPTER 18

Understanding and Knowledge

Over the years, God has revealed *ten helpful keys* for identifying His voice of direction. To clearly identify God's voice, I have learned there are five things a person must *have* and five things a person must *do*. Let's take a look at the first two "must haves".

An Understanding

The first "must have" is quite simple. In order to hear God's voice, you must have the understanding that God wants to direct the details of your life. Proverbs 3:6 reminds us that God wants us to consider what He wants in all the "ways of our day". Unless we understand that God wants to direct the details of our life, we won't be listening for the direction of His Spirit; we won't be looking for Him. Speaking of the Holy Spirit, Jesus said:

> *"The world cannot receive him, because it isn't looking for him and doesn't recognize him. But you know him, because he lives with you now and later will be in you."*

JOHN 14:17

To hear God's voice you must have an understanding that He wants to direct the details of your life.

Knowledge

Secondly, you must have knowledge of the two sources of your thoughts. We said earlier that all thoughts come from two sources. Our thoughts come from the Mind of our Flesh (human wisdom) and from the Mind of Christ (Divine wisdom).

The *Mind of our Flesh* makes decisions and choices on the basis of two things: *Reason and Impulses* that come from its carnal nature. It makes decisions on the basis of what seems *reasonable* and *feels best* at the given time.

Here is what the Bible says about the Mind of the Flesh:

> *Now the mind of the flesh which is **sense** and **reason** without the Holy Spirit is death…That is because the mind of the flesh with its carnal thoughts and purposes is hostile to God, for it does not submit itself to God's Law; indeed it cannot.*
>
> ROMANS 8:6-7 (AMP), emphasis added

In contrast, the direction for decisions we receive from the Mind of Christ (Divine wisdom) does not come as a result of reason or impulses. We receive the direction of God's wisdom as a result of *revelation*. That means God has to reveal His answers to us on the basis of how He thinks because we don't think like He does.

Standing outside of time, God's wisdom has our entire life in view. His wisdom and knowledge are unlimited. A wise person said, "God sees tomorrow and does what is best today." His thoughts are higher than ours. We cannot *reason out* His thinking or His direction because our wisdom is limited.

To accumulate more money, human wisdom will direct us to save it—even hoard it. God's wisdom, in contrast, often directs us to give it away in order to get more. *God's divine wisdom extends beyond our human reason.* Speaking of the mysteries of God's ways, I Corinthians 2:10, 11 & 13 (NKJV) say:

But God has revealed them to us through His Spirit, For the Spirit searches all things, yes, the deep things of God... These things we also speak, not in words which man's wisdom teaches but which the Holy Spirit teaches.

Again, in and of ourselves, we cannot think the way God thinks. There are times when I hear myself say things from a podium I have never thought before. In the moment, God's wisdom *reveals* what He wants me to say. The mind of Christ—Divine wisdom—is based on revelation.

A man's steps are of the Lord; how then can a man understand his own way.

PROVERBS 20:24 (NKJV)

The Bible is God's own revelation of how He thinks. If we want to recognize God's voice, we must know how He thinks. That's why we must spend time reading the Bible every day. And as we read, we must ask the Holy Spirit to unlock the meaning of the words we are reading. Because, again, only the Holy Spirit can reveal God's personal thoughts and ways for us—to us. Very importantly, as we listen for God's voice throughout the day, we must *be prepared for the direction of His wisdom to surpass and therefore defy our human reasoning.*

One snowy winter afternoon, I had scheduled an appointment for a haircut. I was standing in the kitchen, an hour before my appointment, when I clearly heard the Holy Spirit say—through an audible thought—**Leave now.**

Considering it only took 25 minutes to get across town, I began to *reason* that God was directing me to leave early to allow time for a problem I would encounter. Human reason will always want an explanation for what you believe God is asking you to do. Thinking I knew what God was up to, I obeyed what I heard, got in the car, and headed for the salon.

With great relief, I reached my destination without any weather-related problems and found that I was 20 minutes early. Scratching my head at God's purpose, I began looking for a parking place.

Just as I prepared to park, my cell phone rang. Mom had remembered my appointment. Living only ten minutes from the salon, she asked if we could meet after my appointment so she could give me a music CD she believed I'd find very encouraging.

Without ever putting my car in park, I headed for her house. Ten short minutes later, I pulled into her driveway to find her waiting at the door. She smiled, greeted me in her loving way and handed the CD through the window. In turn, I handed her some chocolate candy, thanked her for the music, told her I loved her, and headed back for my appointment.

The trip back was quick and easy. I actually arrived back with two minutes to spare. Best of all, the music she gave me was a tremendous encouragement not just to me, but to the many women I played it for that month at Jesus First Wives Club.

No scripture verse could have directed me to leave early, no circumstance required that I leave early. God revealed His will to me by the Holy Spirit. And His direction *did* surpass my own reason. As an added bonus—God revealed the purpose for His specific direction.

The result? My faith in trusting God's direction was strengthened and tangible needs were met. Again, the Mind of the Flesh operates on reason—to exalt itself. The Mind of Christ operates by revelation—to honor God.

Every thought comes from one of these two sources. Again, the particular thoughts we want to capture and consider are those that *prompt us to action in what we think, do, or say.* Listen for the direction of audible thoughts like these:

+ *Get Started*

+ *Not today*

+ *Offer to help*

+ *Make the appointment now*

+ *Tell the Truth*

+ *Put that back*

+ *Keep quiet*

+ *Rest*

+ *Be Patient*

+ *Stay in this lane*

Again, not all of the thoughts that come from our own understanding—our own human wisdom—are sinful. God does not tell us to disregard our own understanding. Rather, Proverbs 3:5, tells us not to lean on it. We must keep our choices harnessed by the righteous guidelines revealed in the Bible.

Guide me with your laws so that I will not be overcome by evil.

PSALM 119:33

Like an unbridled horse, the carnal power of our flesh's thinking can run us in the opposite direction of God's will, at any time.

For if you live by its dictates, you will die. But if through the power of the Spirit you put to death the deeds of your sinful nature, you will live.

ROMANS 8:13 (NLT)

The Holy Spirit's Presence in us enables us to receive and understand the thoughts of God's will for our individual lives. As The Spirit makes God's will known, we must be ready to surrender the choice of our own human understanding to God's understanding. As we do, each Divine directive gives us the opportunity walk out the deeds of Christ.

The process of being transformed into the wonderful likeness of God's Son all begins with learning how God thinks. That's why it's critical that we spend time in God's Word. As we continue to obey God's Voice, one audible thought at a time, the very character of God will be forged in us. And by God's grace, Jesus, the Son of God, will become visible in us.

CHAPTER 19

Seven Characteristics of the Mind of the Flesh

There is something...deep within me, in my lower nature, that is at war with my mind.

ROMANS 7:23

Let's take a close look at our covert enemy: the Mind of the Flesh. As we have learned, we are born with a carnal mind.

For I was born a sinner—yes, from the moment my mother conceived me.

PSALM 51:5

And Romans 8:7 says our carnal mind:

...is always hostile to God. It never did obey God's laws, and it never will.

For understanding, we are going to liken the Mind of the Flesh to a language. You and I are born speaking flesh. It's our native language. We don't have to study it. We are born with knowledge of it. It is what we understand. Romans 8:6-7 tell us this language speaks out of *sense and reason.*

To illustrate that our native "thinking language" speaks out of sense and reason, I'd like for you to recall times in the past when you've prepared to pay your bills. Have you ever sighed with relief as you added them all up to find you had just enough money to cover them?

If so, maybe you have also experienced that sinking feeling when you suddenly realize you have not allowed money for your tithe to God. If you're like me, the moment you realized it, you probably heard a clear voice that eloquently insisted you be *reasonable.* Surely God wouldn't expect you to give Him money that was already delegated to pay your bills. The voice may have become insistent that you use common *sense* and pay your tithe later—God will understand.

The mind of the flesh will consistently work to *reason us* into disobeying the *revealed* will of God's Word. As we know, it is God's will that we take our tithe off the top of our income—not off the bottom. The language of the flesh speaks first out of sense and reason.

Secondly, according to Romans 8, our "thinking language" speaks out of the impulses of its carnal desires. The language of our flesh says, "Satisfy me." We may reason away paying our tithe to pay a bill but have you ever noticed how fast our selfish flesh will reason away paying a bill to buy some nonessential item we want with the money we don't have? Again, the mind of the flesh, the language of human wisdom, speaks out of reason and the impulses of its carnal desire.

When God chooses to speak to us, we must be prepared for this selfish reasoning of the flesh to push us to take action that is absolutely contrary to the mind of Christ. To quickly identify when our flesh is speaking, to control our decisions, here are seven characteristics of the mind of the flesh.

First: Flesh Doubts God

Many mornings, as I wake up and think about all I have to do, the Holy Spirit faithfully reminds me that His mercy for my day is brand new. Yet, on the heels of His voice, I usually hear another voice.

The voice of my flesh is quick to challenge my hope for receiving God's help. Each morning it also speaks. It has brand new reasons for why I shouldn't expect help from God for the situations I face. How about you? How often do you hear reasons for doubting God will bring change to the difficult circumstances you face?

Every day, the mind of the flesh waits with a new plan for convincing us that God can't be trusted. Trusting a God who isn't visible just doesn't make *sense* to our flesh. Uh-oh, there's that word again. Flesh will fearfully chide us that it's dangerous to make decisions on the basis of someone or something we can't see.

The moment we identify God's voice and determine to obey it, we should expect our flesh's sense, reason, and desire to start its chiding, doubtful discourse. The presence of these doubtful thoughts isn't proof that we don't love God. That presence is proof that we have two minds at war within us. This fact also explains why we can be drawn to God one moment and resist Him the next.

It is critical that we be able to distinguish between the two voices that speak to us. If we can't, we'll vacillate back and forth between belief and unbelief. James 1:5-8 describes this very dilemma of being tossed back and forth between trust and doubt. Here, God warns us that tolerating the process will cause us to become unstable in all our ways; physical aspects of our mental health will suffer.

In contrast, the mind of Christ will urge us to believe what God has said when we can't see anything. That is the essence of faith: obeying without seeing. Most importantly, Hebrews 11:6 reminds us that, without faith, it is impossible to please God. The mind of the flesh doubts God.

Second: Flesh Promotes Fear

Our flesh has one goal: paralyze obedience to God. And to that end fear is the most effective of all tools. Specifically, our flesh attempts to create fear in us by whispering lies to us about the trustworthiness of God's character and plans. In one way or another it suggests that obeying God will always result in personal pain and loss.

It will try to evoke fear with regard to giving to God and others, with statements like these:

"If you let go of what you have—you won't have enough to live on."

"God likes for you to go without—so you'll have to depend on Him."

If we don't recognize the source and ulterior motive behind this "audible taunting", we become fearful and our willingness to give is paralyzed.

Further, flesh speaks fear-provoking words to paralyze our willingness to serve and love others. In case you haven't noticed, our flesh keeps complete files of past offenses and hurts. And it loves to open those files and read them to us. It warns us to expect the same pain and betrayal in the future that people have caused us in the past.

When a former offender extends the smallest olive branch, we hear: "No one really cares about you—you're being used. Guard your heart or you'll be sorry."

When I was a little girl, Mom taught me it was wrong to talk back. In this case, it's not only right—it's critical. The Mind of Christ insists that we stand up to the groundless fears our flesh creates and talk back with truth. As we would say in my children's Sunday school class, we must fight with Scripture.

The Mind of Christ courageously directs us to be vulnerable, to forgive, to expose our heart and everything we own to God's purposes—in spite of the perceived personal cost.

Be assured, God knows how to protect everything we entrust to Him—especially our heart. And He has a great dividend program. With each victory, we find ourselves more courageous and more spiritually impervious to Satan's fear-provoking attacks than we were before. We must anticipate and be prepared for the Mind of the Flesh to attack us by promoting fear.

Third: Flesh Avoids Uncomfortable Circumstances

The voice of our flesh recommends we take the easy way out. It pressures us to twist the truth and lie to get out of things like exercise, difficult conversations and hard commitments we've made with our time and money.

The Mind of Christ, in contrast, calls us to confront difficulty head on. With strength and clear direction, the Holy Spirit urges us forward with words like: *Tell the truth. You CAN handle this. Patience is performing a perfect work in you.* Be prepared for the mind of your flesh to give you reasons to avoid uncomfortable circumstances.

Fourth: Flesh Uses Intelligence and Abilities to Undermine Faith

Our intelligence and abilities have been given to us by God to accomplish His individual purposes while we're on Earth. But they can also fuel our confidence in our own wisdom. *Intelligence produces a surplus amount of reasoning ability.*

Throughout my life, the mind of my flesh has used my intelligence to challenge a radical walk of faith. It has caused me to question God when I should have simply obeyed Him.

> *"unless you...become like little children [trusting, lowly, loving, forgiving], you can never enter the kingdom of heaven at all."*
> MATTHEW 18:3 (AMP)

God uses our intelligence to place us where He wants to use us in the Earth. Chemists, surgeons and rocket scientists utilize the intelligence God has given them to derive answers to the most complex problems we face. But, as we have learned, human intelligence is *incapable* of deriving or 'discerning' God's will. *God's will can only be revealed to us by His Word and His Spirit.*

> *For God in His wisdom saw to it that the world would never find God through human brilliance.*
>
> I CORINTHIANS 1:21

> *If anyone among you seems to be wise in this age, let him become a fool that he may become wise, for the wisdom of this world is foolishness to God.*
>
> I CORINTHIANS 3:18-19 (ESV)

The mind of the flesh uses intelligence and abilities to undermine faith.

Fifth: Flesh Encourages Sin

As we have seen, the audible thoughts of our flesh push us to commit sin: to selfishly hoard what we have, to lie, to steal, to do whatever is necessary to satisfy its own desires. It is a formidable enemy because it lives within us. For that reason, it has the necessary access to influence our behavior at any time. And, as James 1:22 states, its reasoning power can deceive us.

And it deceives us most successfully when its voice mixes truth with error. Often, when the flesh tempts us to sin—to do something we know is wrong—we will hear something like this: "It's your life isn't it? Do whatever you want. Jesus will forgive you—no matter what you do! Have a little fun. You can repent later."

The truth is, each time we purposefully choose to enjoy sin for a season, we run the risk of being enslaved by that sin forever. Have you ever opened a credit card to get a good discount on one item and found yourself paying for other things on that card years later?

> *Don't you realize that you become the slave of whatever you choose to obey? You can be a slave to sin, which leads*

to death, or you can choose to obey God, which leads to righteous living.

ROMANS 6:16 (NLT)

Remember, our carnal mind runs contrary to the righteousness of God. If we discern God's direction and obey it—Walk in the Spirit—we will be protected from sin and its enslaving power. The mind of the flesh encourages sin.

Sixth: Flesh has a Goal to Conform Us to the World

Just as God's Word has the power to transform us into His image, the god of this world has power to conform us to his. The deceptive voice of flesh tells us that we can remain neutral in our daily living, being neither transformed into God's image nor conformed to Satan's.

But Romans 12:2 lists only those two options. There is no "just me" option. There is me, under the influence of God's Spirit and there is me under the influence of the "spirit of this age". Each day, through our obedience to God (or lack of it) we are increasingly reflecting the God of Heaven to others or the god of this world to others. When is the last time you saw Satan in a human face?

The stakes are high. Therefore we should never be surprised at the lengths flesh will go—with reason—to influence our decisions—thereby distorting God's visibility in us.

One sure way it attempts to distort God's visibility in us is by suggesting we compromise Biblical behavior for the sensible sake of peace and unity. Audible thoughts caution us to keep the straight laces of our gospel to ourselves so we don't offend anyone. Yet Romans 9 tells us that Jesus' very existence is an offense.

"The world...hates me because I testify of it that its works are evil."

JOHN 7:7 (NKJV)

Jesus never claimed that He came to bring peace to the earth.

"Do not think that I came to bring peace on earth. I did not come to bring peace but a sword."

MATTHEW 10:34 (NKJV)

And as Christians, He expects that we follow His example; bearing His image, He intends that we pick up the sword that is the Word of God and declare war on sin. Because Christians have forgotten that the Truth offends and divides, the pressure to "fit in" opens many a door to personal sin. Consequently, as was said in an earlier chapter, it's hard to distinguish the behavior of the church from the behavior of the world.

By way of illustration, a chaplain at Baylor University conducted a survey among Baptist newlyweds. His research revealed that only 27% of the churchgoers entered marriage as virgins.[10] That means 73% chose not to be prudish. Needless to say the business of Christian Counseling is booming.

The sobering truth is, with each day's choices, we are being transformed into one of two images. Who do people see when they look at you? The next time a voice whispers that a little sin won't hurt, you and I had better consider whether or not we really want to risk seeing Satan's face when we look in the mirror. The mind of the flesh has a goal. It speaks to conform us to the image of the world.

Seventh: Flesh Provides a Door for Satan's Will

In Mark 8:33 (AMP), we find Peter rebuking Jesus after He said men were going to put him (Jesus) to death. Peter was upset by what Jesus said because he *reasoned* that the gospel his Master was preaching would not survive if Jesus did not. What Jesus had just said did not make *sense* to Peter.

But Jesus recognized the voice behind the words of Peter's flesh and said:

"Get behind me Satan! For you do not have a mind intent on promoting what God wills, but what pleases men."

There is a way that seems right to a man but the end thereof are the ways of death.

PROVERBS 14:12 (KJV)

Jesus did die just as He said He would. And, as a result of the sacrifice God allowed, we can all be reconciled to Him. Additionally, we have triumph over sin in this life and the hope of eternal life to come.

This book is written to help you identify the voices prompting you to action. That ability is critical. Why? Just as the mind of Christ opens the door for God's will, the mind of the flesh opens the door to Satan's.

Be Unreasonable

Today you may be struggling to identify God's voice in the middle of crushing circumstances. If everything seems to be going wrong as you're fighting to do what's right, be encouraged. The will of God, however unreasonable it seems, has you right where you need to be to receive God's best. With each passing day, listen for the Holy Spirit to reveal God's will with audible thoughts that prompt you to action.

And as you wait, remember that your flesh speaks out of reason and the impulses of its carnal nature to influence your decisions. Flesh does not hesitate to use doubt, fear, intelligence, the pleasure of sin, the comfort of compromise, and Satan himself to stop you from obeying God.

In the midst of the confusion, stand fast, remembering that *God's answers and the blessings that go with them are never secured by reason.* In fact, the direction of His Voice usually seems unreasonable.

You might say, "But Marty we need to use reason some times, don't we?" Yes, reason has a place in living responsibly with the choices God gives us. It is reasonable to buy only what we can afford. It is reasonable to go to bed early when we have to get up early. Yet, when God prompts us to action, if necessary, we must be prepared to disregard reason and obey Him by faith. As a wise person has said, the guidance of the Holy Spirit doesn't disregard reason. It just surpasses it.

It was not reasonable for Noah to build a boat when it had never rained. It was not reasonable for Abraham to pack up all of His family and head into the desert, not knowing where to go. It was not reasonable for Daniel to pray, knowing that it meant death. Yet all these heroes of faith rejected reason and obeyed God. What He asked did not need to make sense to them. They knew God and His Word well enough to recognize His voice. May generations to come say the same of us!

CHAPTER 20

A Personal Committment

We have learned the first "must have" for hearing God's voice is the understanding that God wants to speak to us to direct the details of our lives. Secondly, we must have a knowledge of the two sources of all our thoughts. The third "must have" is a critical one. To hear God's voice we must have a personal commitment to a renewed mind.

What is a renewed mind? Very simply, *a renewed mind is a mind saturated with the Word of God.* When we dip a sponge down in a warm sink of soapy suds and lift it out, we'll find that it's saturated—dripping—with water. A renewed mind is one that's saturated with the Word of God.

> *"Study this Book of Instruction continually. Meditate on it day and night so you will be sure to obey everything written in it."*
> JOSHUA 1:8 (NLT)

> *...keep my commands in your heart, for they will prolong your life many years and bring you prosperity.*
> PROVERBS 3:1-2 (NIV)

Yet we have learned that we are born with a carnal mind.

...the mind of the flesh is hostile to God; for it does not submit itself to God's law, indeed it cannot.
ROMANS 8:7 (AMP)

What's the obvious deduction? If we intend to hear and obey God, we must commit to the process of allowing our carnal mind to be renewed. We must submit our thinking—our brain—to the power washing of God's Word.

That He might sanctify and cleanse it with the washing of water by the Word,
EPHESIANS 5:26 (KJV)

If we truly want to be transformed into the likeness of Jesus, we must acknowledge that it starts with the thoughts that trigger what we do and say.

...let God transform you into a new person by changing the way you think. Then you will learn to know God's will for you, which is good and pleasing and perfect.
ROMANS 12:2 (NLT)

Very simply, if we want to recognize God's voice, we must saturate our mind with the written record of *how He thinks*. Then, as we obey what we hear, day-by-day, our mind builds new pathways of thinking, resulting in new and righteous patterns of behavior. If you're sick and tired of dealing with the same failures, that promise from the book of Romans should give you an inspiring breeze of hope.

Modern science bears out this truth of God's Word; thinking patterns of the brain can be changed—renewed. With the medical advances of various scans measuring brain activity, we now know that, at every stage of life, brain cells have the capacity to grow new branches (dendrites) that form new thought pathways.

Our minds can literally be renewed. We can learn to think like Jesus thinks. And there is no greater thrill on Earth than that of watching God use our transformed thinking and behavior to touch people in a way that we know is beyond our capabilities.

Building A Library

We have said that our mind becomes renewed as we saturate it with how God thinks and as we collect truth about God. We can compare the process of renewing our mind, then, to building a library. This comparison is fitting since our physical brain actually contains a library, where our knowledge of God can be stored. Did you know your brain files, in categories, a memory of everything your senses take in? That includes a memory of everything we touch, smell, taste, see, and hear. This library has enough storage capacity to record 11 million books.

Dr. Don Colbert, a Christian expert in the science of nutrition, says, "Just as your family room (or kitchen) is the center of activity for your family…your brain has a memory-central also. The limbic system…is its main memory center…(and it) is composed of five main divisions…. Just as an efficient secretary stores important information in organized files and cabinets, your brain does the same. After your memories are processed and sorted…they are sent to storage facilities."[11]

Here are three of those storage divisions.

Long-term memories are stored in the neo-cortex division of the limbic system (gray matter). The memories stored here include any information that's been memorized, repeated to us frequently, carefully studied, or lived out.

Short-term memories are stored in the hippocampus division of the limbic system. Memories stored here include phone numbers we use once, mental lists, and names such as those of people who help us at call centers or restaurants. This short term information doesn't get filed away. Our brain knows that the data it is receiving at the time isn't going to be necessary in the future, so it deletes it immediately after it's used. (We are certainly fearfully and wonderfully made!)

Finally, emotionally charged memories—those captured during times of extreme excitement or trauma are processed and stored in the amygdala division of our limbic system. All that our senses take in is stored in this library of our mind. And this information can be quickly recalled, as our brain cells interact with each other at lightning speed.

As you recognize the need to renew your mind, build a library of how God thinks by making the Word of God your primary resource. During your personal study time, read your Bible first. It's very important because the Bible is the supreme authority in revealing who God is, to us.

God is eager to reveal Himself to us. And God uses our library to do it. The larger our library, the more detailed God's conversation with us will be. Each of us can have as large a library as we are willing to build.

With all this talk about a library, by now you may be wondering where books for our library come from (other than the Bible). We bind a new book for the library of our knowledge of God each time we memorize a Scripture verse or learn a new principle from God's Word. And we can gain these new principles in a variety of ways.

In addition to reading the Bible, we can gain a principle (a book) by listening to sermons or reading Christian authors. We can learn new principals through any form of social media; through online teaching, podcasts, Christian radio, television or film. Certainly we can learn new truth about God through our fellowship with other believers.

One of my favorite ways to absorb truth about God or refresh my spirit is through the words of songs and hymns. Everything is easier to remember when it's set to rhythm or music. As a preacher's daughter, I sang every song in all the hymnals hundreds of times.

To this day, I'm still amazed by my recall of the words to countless hymns my library has filed away. I can still remember words to songs I haven't sung for twenty years or more. The next time you're discouraged, read the words of the hymn, "A Mighty Fortress Is Our God." Indeed, every song we memorize is bound into a book for our library.

You surround me with songs.

PSALM 32:7

Again, if we want what we learn about God to stay in the long-term memory division of our brain, we must review it, memorize it, study it or apply it in daily living. As we do, what we've recently learned becomes a book for the very real library of our mind. The more we learn, the richer our library becomes.

Oh, the depth of the riches both of the wisdom and knowledge of God!

ROMANS 11:33 (NKJV)

Again, if we merely hear the information, it will be deleted in the short-term division of our library. Maybe you, like me, can remember hearing inspiring messages from Pastors, only to have trouble telling someone else what you heard hours later.

But be ye doers of the word, and not hearers only.

JAMES 1:22 (KJV)

Regarding this war we are called to fight as Christians—are you in it to win it? Are you intentionally living to accomplish God's purposes for your life on the earth?

I ask because accomplishing God's purposes requires a renewed mind. And building a library—working to acquire a renewed mind—takes strategic *effort and discipline*. You know that's the truth if you've ever tried to simply be faithful in having personal time with God every day.

Plainly stated, when we make a personal commitment to renew our mind, we should be prepared for a fight. Flesh always prefers watching TV to reading the Bible. Flesh prefers carnal knowledge to truth. If you doubt that, consider how easily your attention is drawn to the sensational material on any printed page, computer screen, television program, or magazine cover.

The mind of the flesh relentlessly lures us to absorb lies—to bind books—from this fallen world's view and fill our library with them. Why? Because Satan wants to do the same thing God wants to do—*build and use our library to direct our behavior.*

One of the gifts Jesus died to give us was that of a free choice. We are completely free to spend our leisure time reading secular novels. We are free to go to the decent movies that only have a minimal amount of sex and murder. We can use our gift of choice to relax with the easy listening music that celebrates this world's idea of love if we choose to. But we need to be prepared. Prepared for what? Prepared for God's rejection? No. Nothing we ever do will change the passionate feelings of love God has for us.

Rather, we need to be prepared for spirits of darkness—through the instrument of our flesh—to pull out and play anything and everything our mind has recorded. And they will play every last refrain, frame, word and picture perfectly, all with the intent of directing our behavior to some level of self-destruction.

Specifically, a favorite target for spirits of darkness is the Christian marriage relationship. They love to hit the rewind button on scenes from movies and TV programs we've watched. They enjoy pulling up the words from songs we've heard, sung or hummed all day and use them to stir up discontent. While humming an oldie favorite, don't be surprised when you hear with your inside ears, "You sure aren't loved like that."

All of a sudden, without warning, like ignorant pawns we're provoking arguments with people we love and doing things we're ashamed of. I can remember more than one time when my behavior was driven by the lies of a single song on the radio.

Some movies openly suggest that sex is an acceptable part of every unmarried love relationship. Further, they suggest that sensual passion is the key to happily ever after. If you've ever had sex outside of marriage you know it doesn't open the door to a fairy tale. It's far more accurate to say that unmarried sex splinters your very soul, with consequences that make it hard to love yourself and harder yet to love others.

I'm finished with the conflict of being blindsided by thoughts that come from a fresh intake of how the world thinks. By God's grace, I choose, daily, to pack my mind with knowledge of God so that His thoughts are constantly flooding my mind; giving me power to walk in the Spirit and sidestep pitfalls of sin.

Many people say I'm radical in my approach. Maybe I am, but I know what I want. I want the passion of my love relationship with Jesus to increase. I want people to see God in me and not the devil. I want to spend the energy of my life on eternal pursuits that pay dividends no man can take from me.

And for those very wonderful reasons, I regularly choose to listen to music that honors God. I choose not to go movies that flaunt the sin Jesus died to free me from. I choose to read books that proclaim God's truth. And with the exception of the news, at God's direction, I watch little television. It's almost impossible to even change channels without defiling yourself and grieving God with pictures of sex, mutilating violence, and witchcraft.

If you and I are going to look like Jesus, it will not be by accident. The transformation takes place one day at a time as we choose to do the work God's grace has made possible. It happens as we exert our will and choose to saturate our minds with knowledge of God.

Who can fathom the opportunity that is ours? The God of Heaven invites us to capture His very own thoughts. And as we obey them, He invites us to watch in the mirror as, day by day, our former image transforms into the image of His own Son!

Spoken Truth—New and Known

When God speaks to us, revealing His immediate will, we see that He uses words of truth from two categories. He may use words of truth that are completely new to us or words of truth we already know. Believers are allowed to know the thoughts of God's will, by His Word and by His Spirit.

> *"Who can know the Lord's thoughts?"…we understand these things, for we have the mind of Christ.*
>
> I CORINTHIANS 2:16 (NLT)

As we have learned, God is eager for us to know His thoughts so He can use our time, resources and energy to accomplish the desires of His will.

I illustrated how God reveals His will to us with new information in the story that involved putting $100.00 in my son's wallet. The amount I was to give was not recorded in the Bible. By listening to God's voice, I gave my son what God wanted him to have. And later, God allowed me to see the purpose of His direction—strengthening my resolve to listen even more intently.

Finally, God reveals His immediate will with words of truth we already know. This is where our library comes in! In His perfect timing, God directs the Holy Spirit (who resides in our spirit) to speak to us by drawing to our conscious mind a Scripture verse or Biblical principle we learned or committed to memory (a book from our library).

> *"But the helper, the Holy Spirit, whom the Father will send in My name, He will teach you all things and bring to your remembrance all things, that I said to you."*
>
> JOHN 14:26 (NKJV)

This is why the size—the richness—of our library is so important. The more our library contains, the more specific

God's direction to us can be. Personally, in times of fear, the Holy Spirit reaches into my library and pulls out a Bible verse—a book that has been bound and placed on the shelf—that reads like this:

I will fear no evil for Thou art with me.

PSALM 23:4 (KJV)

God cannot speak to us with Scripture we haven't learned. At least 80% of all the Scripture that God uses to direct my speaking and writing comes from the library built in me as child. Growing up, I recited verses for a Bible memory program that rewarded me with prizes through the mail.

What about your children or grandchildren's library? What are they watching, hearing and learning throughout the day? What music is being bound into books for the shelves of their young minds? What videos and television programs are they watching with your blessing? How will God speak to them in the decision making years of their life, if no one is working to see that Scripture is being stored on the shelves of their heart? We have much to do for those we love and for ourselves.

Are you committed to the renewing of your mind? Be listening for the audible thoughts of God's voice. God will help you with an attainable game plan. Amid all our responsibilities God encourages us on and gives us His enabling grace.

Recently, while enduring some discouraging thoughts brought on by weariness, God the Father told the Holy Spirit to encourage me by using the words of a song stored in my library. The words might encourage you. Regardless of what you're facing at this moment, God wants you to know, "It will be worth it all, when we see Jesus."

CHAPTER 21

A Wholly Submitted Heart

The fourth "must have" for experiencing intimate conversation with God is a complete trust in Him; a wholly submitted heart.

If you want favor with both God and man...then trust the Lord completely, don't ever trust yourself.

PROVERBS 3:5

The Terrible Truth

It's not hard to hear God's voice. That statement surprises many people at first. Who wouldn't want to hear God's voice? Often times, us.

If you doubt that's true, the next time you really want something—for yourself or someone else—something to eat, something new to wear, drive, or live in, a relationship or physical change, stop and notice how difficult it is to let that desire go easily. Our flesh is masterful at deceiving us. It keeps us from seeing how much control we reserve, for our personal satisfaction and happiness.

If we sincerely want to hear God's voice, we have to start by acknowledging that a follower of Jesus is someone whose life is *wholly yielded to God's control.* Since that is true, it's important to stop and honestly acknowledge how submitted your heart is. How much do you really want God's will to prevail in the details of your life?

The only difficult part about hearing God's voice is *wanting to hear Him.*

"If any man desires to do His will (God's pleasure), he will know—have the needed illumination to recognize and tell for himself—whether the teaching is from God..."

JOHN 7:17 (AMP)

Disintegrating Doubts

Since a wholly submitted heart is necessary for hearing God speak, let's consider how we can obtain and maintain one. First, to obtain a wholly submitted heart we must identify personal obstacles of doubt.

I was 23 years old when I had a head-on collision with my inability to fully trust God. I'm not big on dredging up the past, but sometimes looking back is the only way to go forward in gaining the freedom that comes from forgiving yourself for past mistakes.

Having looked back, I now understand exactly how Satan succeeded in convincing me that God's will was something to be feared. How about you? Have you ever feared God's will? More importantly, have you ever stopped to ask yourself why? How will you and I ever learn to trust God completely if we don't stop to consider why we've struggled to trust Him at all?

Ironically, Satan dismantled my faith in God's goodness as I sat attentively in church week after week. In short, He used the testimonies of the faithful missionaries I mentioned, who suffered for the gospel's sake. And he launched his lies when I was the most vulnerable; in the innocence of my youth when I was too young to defend my own heart with Truth.

As I looked toward my own future, I connected Satan's unholy dots and reasoned that saying yes to God was saying yes to a life of painful sacrifice with zero satisfaction. And I believed that lie as a result of hearing far more about the *price* of submitting to God than the *reward* of it.

From a young age, I watched devoted followers of Jesus make great sacrifices for the sake of the gospel without understanding that God's grace—His supernatural power—was flowing lavishly to them. At the time, I couldn't see that His own, loving Presence made His purposes for their life well worth the price they seemed to pay. Again, I didn't hear much about the reward of their faith and I certainly couldn't see that their lives were deeply satisfying. After they shared their stories, they left the country. How I wish those who challenged me to seek God's will had placed equal emphasis on the lavish grace of God that accompanies His will.

It is critical that you and I give people the complete picture when we're walking through hard times. In addition to sharing our prayer requests for strength, we should also share the amazing accounts of God's nearness and provision in the difficult times we've already come through. Why don't we do that more often? I believe it's because our troublemaking flesh fills us with the fear that sharing our accounts of God's sustaining power will make people think we don't need them. We fear people will neglect to give us the attention or assistance we think we need.

God is the source of our strength. As we give Him credit for sustaining us, He will continue to supply all we need—from people and their pantries. And He will use our testimony to create courage in others who struggle.

Let the redeemed of the Lord say so,…

PSALM 107:2 (NKJV)

Satan always succeeds in creating obstacles for our faith when he gets us to focus on partial truth—in my case—I focused on the partial truth that obedience to God results in pain. And a partial truth is a whole lie!

Unfortunately, because Satan succeeded in drawing my attention to only the *price* of obedience, I made the early conscious decision to trust God with my salvation but not with my dreams. I took myself out of the race the Apostle Paul talks about.

I would not be competing for the prize of the High Calling. Instead, I'd take the safe route. No chancy sacrifice here. I'd walk by my own sight rather than run in blind faith and risk being unhappy. Who knows? Maybe I'd get a consolation prize for clean living.

Consequently, two years later, with love, marriage and the baby carriage—my way, life had become quite stressful. While my husband worked undercover narcotics, I worked to be "The Total Woman"—which was harder than I anticipated, with a two year old and an infant.

Fiercely determined, I wore myself out every day by relying on my strength and abilities to make my dreams come true. As an "almost" completely committed Christian, I had daily devotions and attended church regularly. And I told God He was certainly free to have His way in my life, as long as He left my dreams for love and happiness alone.

Because divorce had ravaged even our parsonage, all I wanted was to remain married to the man I loved and live happily ever after. At the mature age of 23, I was in control and losing control.

Today, after 50 plus years of living, I have seen that there are two things that will instantly disintegrate obstacles of doubt and force us to fully submit our hearts to God. The first one is the complete exhaustion of our personal strength—the final realization that, for all our striving, we are incapable of securing our own happiness. The second experience that fosters our submission is a crisis so intense we immediately recognize God is our only hope.

Mercifully, at 23, both of these things happened to me. By personally trying to escape the pain and unhappiness I feared God's will would bring, I created my own. How sad it is that many only submit to the God who loves them, as a last resort?

Broken and hopeless, I clearly remember saying, "God, I'm finally ready to trust you with everything." In tears and exhaustion, I inched my way over the crags of my reasoning, to the ledge of my own human understanding. And in full faith, I leaped. I jumped into the waiting arms of the One who actually did love me to death. If it were possible to hear the sound a heart makes when it leaps in faith, I'm sure you would have heard my mine say, "Geronimo!"

Amazingly, as I have said, that very same week, God began to teach me how to hear His voice.

The Lord is good and glad to teach the proper path to all who go astray; He will teach the ways that are right and best to those who humbly turn to him, every path He guides us on is fragrant with His loving kindness and His truth.

PSALM 25:8-10

Most Christians don't hear the voice of the Holy Spirit speaking to them because (knowingly or unknowingly) they don't want to hear Him speak. Solomon, the wisest man who ever lived, knew even he needed help to desire God's will.

"May He give us the desire to do His will in everything, and to obey all the commandments and instructions He has given our ancestors. And may these words of my prayer be constantly before Him day and night, so that He helps me...in accordance with our daily needs."

I KINGS 8:58-59

For it is God which worketh in you both to will and to do of His good pleasure.

PHILIPPIANS 2:13 (KJV)

We struggle to desire God's will because our flesh wants control over our life and dreams. And ironically we fight to maintain this control when, more often than not, God has given us the very dreams we fear losing control of.

God will not speak if we don't want His will. The main hurdle to clear in order to gain a clear knowledge of God's will is the simple desire for it. How about you? In the middle of your current struggle, it's time for gut-level honesty. Do you really want God's resolution to the situation you're facing?

If you hesitate at all with your answer, let me ask you another question. Is it possible that Satan has created some obstacle of doubt that keeps you from trusting God completely? Is there some hurt you wrongly hold God responsible for? Is there something or someone you care so much about that you are unwilling to submit it or them (and therefore yourself) completely to God? If you really want to know what it is that holds you back from trusting completely, God will reveal it to you. Ask Him and prepare yourself.

The instant we bow in full submission to God, it is "spirit natural" for Him to flood our spirit with an awareness of His Presence and the knowledge of His will. Is that what you want?

Jesus answered, "...If a person [really] loves Me, he will keep My word—obey My teaching; and My Father will love him, and We will come to him and make Our home (abode, special dwelling place) with him."

JOHN 14:23 (AMP)

The only thing that can separate us from God is our distrust of Him. Solomon said in Proverbs 1:7 that the first step in gaining wisdom—God's thought process—is to trust Him. The great apostle Paul said:

I have given up everything else. I have found it to be the only way to really know Christ.

PHILIPPIANS 3:10

To hear God's voice, you must have a wholly submitted heart. To have a wholly submitted heart you must identify any personal obstacles of doubt and overcome them with truth.

Now, a wholly submitted heart is certainly not a perfect heart. Surrender is an ongoing process. Rather, a wholly submitted heart is one that stands ready and willing to release control to God as God reveals it is necessary.

Will you take a few moments to quiet your own heart before the living God and ask Him to reveal any obstacle, any hurt, any passion, standing between you and a wholly submitted heart? If you ask God, He will reveal the truth to you. And if you surrender what you have withheld, God, will flood your heart and mind with the direction of His glorious will.

Two Ways To Maintain A Submitted Heart

God is Great—God is Good...

Once attained, we must work to maintain a wholly submitted heart. The first step? We must be completely convinced that God is good. Are you? If you struggle with this basic truth, it's important to figure out—again—what Satan has used in your life to distort your view of God. You and I will never be able to trust God with the details of our life if we don't believe that He is good.

The only way to dismantle and rebuild your belief system about God is by the process of Scripture memory. As we have learned, the written Word of God has living power that man will never be able to explain. When Satan attacks the foundational truth of God's goodness, we must talk back to him, just as Jesus did, with a Bible verse we've memorized. And we must say it as often as we need to.

...He is my shelter. There is nothing but goodness in Him.

PSALM 92:15

Undoubtedly, Satan's most effective strategy for getting us to doubt God's goodness is his continual emphasis on the existence of pain. Many walk away from belief in God as a result of the suffering they see around them.

Yet the reality that any breaking of God's law results in pain hardly makes Him responsible for the sin that causes our pain. God is not the author of our pain. Pain comes from the three sources of sin.

First: Hebrews 3:12 and Galatians 6:7 tell us that pain comes from the poor choices of our own flesh.

Second: I Thessalonians 2:14 and I Peter 3:17 tell us that pain comes from the poor choices of others (that affect us).

And third: Romans 5:12 tells us that pain comes from this sin-cursed world.

We experience the ravages of natural disasters and disease because we live on a planet that spins under the curse of sin. Pain comes from the poor choices of our own flesh, the poor choices of others, and this sin-cursed world.

Instead of being the Author of our pain, Romans 8:28 reveals God to be the Director of our pain. As we submit to His purposes, God commits to direct our difficult circumstances and redeem the very pain sin has caused; using it to bring us blessing. Now *that's* a 'win—win' proposition.

You must be convinced that God is good. If you're not, you will never fully submit your heart to Him; thereby making it futile for God to entrust you with the direction of His will.

For truly, let not such a person imagine that he will receive anything [he asks for] from the Lord, [For being as he is] a man of two minds—hesitating, dubious, irresolute,...

JAMES 1:7-8 (AMP)

Are you convinced that God is good?

A Packed Picnic Basket

Secondly, to maintain a wholly submitted heart, you and I must accept God's preordained plan for our daily provision. Our great need for security causes us to wrongly believe that we have a right to see the future. We want to see before we believe. And when we can't see the specific resources God will use to provide for tomorrow's needs, we struggle to trust Him with tomorrow's needs. Yet Jesus said, in Matthew 6 (AMP):

"Therefore I tell you, stop being perpetually uneasy (anxious and worried) about your life, what you shall eat or what you shall drink; or about your body, what you shall put on... your heavenly Father knows well that you need them all...So do not worry or be anxious about tomorrow."

These words in Matthew make it quite plain that God expects us to trust Him for our needs to be met, one day at a time. Yet how quickly we travel from faith to doubt. With a few minutes of news, we fear losing our income. With a magazine picture, we fear getting older. With an ache, we fear losing our health. With a cross word, we fear loneliness. What if—what if—what if?

Our needs may be great, due to loss of finances, failing health or even physical abandonment. Nonetheless, we have no right to doubt God because He won't show us the future. Whether we want to admit it or not, it's waiting on God to supply our needs that reveals His reality. It's waiting on God day by day that teaches us to trust Him.

When I whimper and question God about tomorrow, He always asks, *"Marty, did you have everything you needed today?"* To my sheepish answer, 'yes', He typically finishes the conversation by saying, *"And you will have everything you need tomorrow."*

God's provision is rich. If we intend to enjoy it, we must accept the fact that His promise of supply—for everything we need from food to hope—comes in increments of 24 hours; in the fenced corral we call today.

Growing up, my children had horses as 4-H projects. I shook my head as I watched those horses strain to get their heads through the slats of the fence where they were corralled, as though the grass on their side just wasn't enough.

Satan knows that if we look back over all God has faithfully brought us through, we find undeniable evidence that God can be trusted to meet our needs. Consequently, he purposely tempts us to look ahead—beyond the boundary of God's promised provision. Faithfulness is God's character. You can no more separate God from His faithfulness than you can separate the sun from its light.

Rest assured, like a great picnic basket, on the threshold of each new day God's satisfying provision sits, packed and waiting, to supply our every need. And it will be packed and ready, tomorrow. Delightful. Anyone hungry for breakfast?

Great is His faithfulness; His mercies begin afresh each morning.

LAMENTATIONS 3:23

CHAPTER 22

A Willingness to Stand

The final "must have" for hearing God's voice is a willingness to *stand through any pain caused to our flesh* by following the Holy Spirit's direction. The battle raging between Jesus, the Prince of Life, and Satan, the Prince of Darkness, is a real one. It is not a figment of spiritual imagination nor is it a figurative expression for the difficulties we encounter in this life. To compound the threat, we (as soldiers) live in reasoning bodies of flesh that naturally oppose God's revealed will. Therefore, our flesh will always experience some discomfort when we obey the orders God gives us. Expect it. It's easy to say we care about others, but just let God ask us to stop what we're doing to help Him encourage another person and listen to how our flesh whines.

We can make an eternal, life-changing difference in the great battle for souls. And we can receive all the satisfaction and rich reward that goes with it. But, if we intend to, we have to be prepared to stand through whatever pain God's direction causes our flesh.

The Case for Grace

To render me ineffective for God, Satan not only caused me to doubt that God's will would satisfy my heart, he caused me to fear the pain of obeying God's will. We must make up our minds whether or not we really believe that there is such a thing as amazing grace—a power from God—beyond ourselves, that enables us to supernaturally endure what His will allows.

If we believe His grace will be sufficient, we will have the courage to obey when what He asks is difficult. If we doubt this grace actually exists, we will run from His will. There is no reason for God to entrust us with the specific direction of His voice if He knows we are too fearful to obey what we hear.

A Small Price to Pay

The pain we face for Jesus' sake varies in degree. God's direction may simply ask that we stand through small disappointments; like the kind we feel when we're packed up and anxious to go ahead with plans and hear God say, *Not today.*

Other times God may ask us to stand through the small pain of embarrassment we sometimes feel as He pursues the lost through us. By the way, in keeping with His heart, much of the activity God's voice prompts us to take involves redemption for someone. One example of His desire to express His love through me took place at the drive-through window of a restaurant near my home.

One busy day, I turned into a fast food parking lot to grab some lunch. When it was my turn to order, I pulled up to the kiosk and politely ordered a small coke and a hamburger (no cheese—that was my attempt to accomplish the eating healthy part).

I dug in my wallet for change and pulled my car around the building. As I edged forward, I heard, *Tell the boy at the window I love him.*

Uh oh. I know that voice. Frozen in disbelief, I also heard, "If you sit really still God might not ask you again."

Obviously, that idea was my flesh's wishful thinking because God did ask me again. And He repeated what He said the first time, *I want you to tell that boy I love him.*

Petrified, I spoke back. "But Lord, I'm sure I'm old enough to be his mother. How is that going to sound?"

Heaven was silent. I knew God meant business. Briefly, I considered my option to disobey. I could just say thank you and drive away. But I knew I'd be miserable for days. I couldn't directly disobey God.

It was my turn. Slowly (believe me—very slowly) I pulled forward and sheepishly looked up into the window to see the face of the one to whom God was determined to express His love. A stocky teenage boy about 16 years old looked back at me. With all the cheer I could muster, I said, "Hello."

"Hello," he replied and took the money I handed him. Knowing I had barely another second before I would have to move up to the next window, I blurted out, "Has anybody told you lately that they loved you?"

A small grin crept across his face and he slightly shook his head no. I charged ahead in a flurry. "Well, I want you to know that Jesus loves you and so do I!"

He smiled. "Thank you."

I pulled forward, sighed with relief, grabbed my white paper bag, and drove away. For all my dread, it really didn't hurt a bit.

The truth is, the lost we pray for every night surround us through the day. They serve us through fast food windows, stand with us in checkout lanes, and sit beside us on airplanes. At a glance, we can see that they are hurting and we can hear in their words that most have no idea who Jesus is.

Yet the pain of embarrassment can cause us to close our eyes to their need and pray that somebody else, with more courage or more time than we have, will share the gospel with them and meet their needs.

We must never underestimate God's ability to bring change to a desperate life through our simple acts of obedience. With a kind word, a compliment offered to a total stranger, a short note of thanks dropped in a mailbox, a few dollars or a loving act of service—even to one who clearly doesn't deserve it—God can transform a human heart. He doesn't need much. With a small boy's lunch, Jesus fed 5,000 hungry people.

Sometimes the pain we are asked to stand through is far greater than the discomfort of embarrassment. I am familiar with pain in many degrees. I know how it feels to stand through the fear and pain associated with a personal diagnosis of cancer, when a routine office visit reveals it. Deeper yet, I know how it feels to be alone and face an uncertain personal future. After twenty-four years, I'm still waiting in peace, today, for God to direct His conclusion to my life story.

I cannot deny that there is a price for following Jesus. But I am qualified to say that the price is infinitely small when compared to the sense of complete fulfillment that living for God's love provides. I'm living in the ashes of many broken dreams. But, one by one, God is replacing them with new ones.

As someone currently living in the nest of their greatest fear—in the set of circumstances they always hoped most to avoid—I have never been more content. After many years of standing in this difficult place, it is still true that I am the most satisfied person I know.

This book has been written so that you too can know the God of Heaven as your intimate companion.

Friendship with God is reserved for those who reverence Him. With them alone, He shares the secrets of His promises.

PSALM 25:14

Two Truths for Standing

Two comforting truths continue to enable me to stand through pain. The first is this: God never calls anyone to battle in this life without suiting and empowering them for it. No one has been more surprised than I at how perfectly suited I am for the fight God has called me to. But the strength seen in me is not mine. To empower us to stand, God indwells us Himself. Wonder of wonders!

To engage His power, all God asks is that we simply relinquish our will to His. That's it. How He loves to put His glorious power on display in mortal beings—weak as we are.

But He said to me, "my grace is enough for you for my power is made perfect in weakness."

II CORINTHIANS 12:9 (NIV)

The second comforting truth is this: painful moments become tolerable as we choose to concentrate on the prize. Paul said:

For our light and momentary troubles are achieving for us an eternal glory that far outweighs them all.

II CORINTHIANS 4:17 (NIV)

I have finally learned enough about Heaven to see that it is worth living for. Not only is Heaven ahead, God has rich rewards for our obedience here!

*Jesus said, "Truly I say to you, there is no one who has left house or brothers or sisters or mother or father or children or farms, for My sake and for the gospel's sake, but that he will receive a hundred times as much **now** in the present age,... along with persecutions; and in the age to come, eternal life."*

MARK 10:29-30 (NAS), emphasis added

Never fear the pain of following God's direction. Paul, who knew a thing or two about standing through pain, said,

Stand steady, and don't be afraid of suffering for the Lord. Bring others to Christ. Leave nothing undone that you ought to do.
II TIMOTHY 4:5

As you stand in obedience, you will see for yourself that God's amazing grace holds securely. And, day-by-day, courage to do His will replaces any fear of it.

"I have told you these things, so that in Me you may have perfect peace and confidence. In the world you have tribulation and trials and distress and frustration; but be of good cheer —take courage, be confident, certain, undaunted—for I have overcome the world.—I have deprived it of power to harm, have conquered it [for you]."
JOHN 16:33 (AMP)

Until we see Jesus, all of us will struggle to maintain a submitted heart. But as our conversation with God increases, our increased love will decrease our doubts about His good purposes! When you are truly in love, there are no fearful areas of distrust. The nature of love is trust. Love compels us to jump in and do whatever it asks.

There is no fear in love;
I JOHN 4:18 (KJV)

Take it from me, any pain you encounter on the road of obedience to God will become for you what it has become for me: a small price to pay for such a Great Love. Try it. You'll like it. I promise. More importantly—God promises!

Those who trust in the Lord are steady as Mount Zion, unmoved by any circumstance.
PSALM 125:1

CHAPTER 23

Five Things You Must Do to Hear God's Voice

It's been necessary to lay a strong foundation to insure you make stable decisions in taking the practical steps that follow. These steps help you clearly identify when God is speaking to you through the internally audible thoughts of your mind.

I will bless the Lord who has counseled me; indeed, my mind instructs me in the night.

PSALMS 16:7 (NAS)

Because every decision has far-reaching consequences, it is critical that we periodically check to see that our hearts remain wholly submitted to God's plans. Ask yourself often: How much do I really want God's will in the details of my life today? Am I willing, at every point, to lay my plans down and exchange them for His?

Lord don't let me make a mess of things. If you will only help me to want your will, then I will follow your laws ever more closely.

PSALMS 119:31-32

David said in Psalms 51:12, "...make me willing to obey you."

For Christians, *wanting* God's will is the only requirement necessary for receiving direction from God. I think that statement may be the most powerful truth this book contains. Everything else is important. But that truth is the key to the door of Divine direction. Again James 1:5, says:

If you want to know what God wants you to do, ask Him, and He will gladly tell you, for He is always ready to give a bountiful supply of wisdom to all who ask Him...

We have just learned that to hear God's voice there are five "must-haves":

(1) An *understanding* that He wants to speak

(2) The *knowledge* of the two sources of your thoughts

(3) A *commitment* to a renewed mind

(4) A wholly *submitted heart* and finally

(5) A *willingness to stand* through pain

Now that we know the five must-haves necessary for hearing God's voice, it's time to cover the five things *we must do* to hear Him speak. At first glance, the following steps may seem too elementary to be mentioned. But the experience of a lifetime proves their importance is understated. Each one plays an important role in aligning the human soul and spirit to receive direction from God. This chapter contains the first four.

To hear God speak, we must:

[1] Verbally Commit Control of Each Day to God.

Accountability is important. I can't stress enough the importance of forming the verbal habit of releasing control of your day to God. When you choose to consciously, verbally tell God the day belongs to Him, you put yourself on record before Heaven. I have seen that

God honors this verbal record of mine with a heightened attentiveness to His direction.

I have set the LORD always before me; because He is at my right hand I shall not be moved.

PSALM 16:8 (NKJV)

You may wake up to a full plate of established plans. You may have a handwritten list of responsibilities you are obligated to accomplish. You may have the precious little free time of a weekend or day off. Regardless, put yourself on record with God, by giving control of the day to Him—before the activity of your day begins. Before my feet touch the floor in the morning, I choose to tell God that it's His day.

"He awakens me morning by morning, He awakens my ear to hear as the learned."

ISAIAH 50:4 (NKJV)

Once you have committed your day to God, soundly expect your flesh to fight to hang on to control of it! You will probably hear thoughts like this one: *"If you let God control your day, there won't be any time left for what's important to you."*

When my flesh creates a sense of panic over releasing control of my day to God, I instantly regain my sense of peace by stopping in my tracks and asking myself, "What is so important to me, today, that I am unwilling to entrust it to God? Is there actually some accomplishment or opportunity that is so valuable to me that I am willing to trade God's plan for it?"

Commit everything you do to the Lord, trust Him to help you do it and He will.

PSALMS 37:5

I have yet to release control of even one day to God without seeing Him provide some blessing beyond my ability to provide to someone else. And, as a divine thank you, He supernaturally assists me in completing the important responsibilities on my existing list.

[2] Get Clean so You Can Receive His Direction

Apart from speaking to us to point out a sin we have committed, God will not speak to us throughout the day if we are tolerating known sin in our heart.

> *If I regard iniquity in my heart, the Lord will not hear.*
>
> PSALM 66:18 (NKJV)

> *"Now we know that God does not hear sinners; but if anyone is a worshiper of God and does His will, He hears Him."*
>
> JOHN 9:31 (NKJV)

Jesus died to pay the price for every sin we have committed and every sin we ever will commit. As we mature in our faith, by reading and doing God's Word, God's power increases in us. And as it does, we experience more and more victory over sins we have given in to before.

Yet only when we see Jesus will we be completely like Him—sinless. In this life, we will commit sin.

> *And there is not a single man in all the Earth who is always good and never sins.*
>
> ECCLESIASTES 7:20

> *If we say that we have no sin, we deceive ourselves, and the truth is not in us.*
>
> I JOHN 1:8 (NKJV)

Sin will not cause God's Presence to leave a true Christian. But it will prohibit His Spirit from communicating with them. That's why we must get clean, as soon as the Holy Spirit convicts us of sin. We do that by acknowledging our behavior as sin, expressing our genuine sorrow for it, and then accepting God's forgiveness.

> *If we confess our sin, He is faithful and just to forgive us our sin and to cleanse us from all unrighteousness.*
>
> I JOHN 1:9 (NKJV)

Once we are clean, communication is instantly restored. And we can joyfully expect to receive His guidance throughout the day.

[3] Get Focused by Spending Time in the Word

God's revealed Word does not require that we read and pray a set amount of time each day. Clearly, some stages of life provide more time than others. My Mom remembers that when my sisters and I were small, her devotions consisted of a Bible verse propped up in the kitchen window. Your objective is to spend some time in God's Word so that He can speak to you and establish your focus. If we need fresh food each day for our temporary physical bodies to be strong, we certainly need fresh food for our eternal soul and spirit to be strong!

Having some system—regardless of how routine—will help you create the habit of beginning the day with the Word. Speaking of routines, some people read a chapter from the book of Proverbs each day because there are thirty-one of them.

As you give God the opportunity to establish your focus with His Word, you will be amazed at how precisely He addresses the current activity of your life. You will also find yourself well prepared with the truth and encouragement you need to keep pressing on.

One day my then four-year-old grandson Caleb was out in the back yard with my other grandchildren. I stood beside him and played with his brown curls while he stood watching the horses in my neighbor's pasture.

In a matter of minutes, the wind picked up and all the horses began running for the barn. I looked over my shoulder to see that, in fact, a large bank of dark purple clouds was quickly moving toward the house. Bits of leaves and sticks began swirling on the ground like tiny wind-up toys. It was time to stop playing and head for the house. I warned the children to grab their toys and began herding them toward the back door.

Just as I did, Caleb abruptly planted his feet and curiously looked up at me with his brown eyes. With his curls blowing he asked, "How do the horses know a storm is coming, when it hasn't even started raining yet?"

I quickly replied, "God tells them—let's go!"

That was good enough for him. And he hurried on toward the house.

The next day, I sat down in my regular spot to start my daily devotions, I asked the Holy Spirit the same question I always ask, "Lord, where do you want me to start my reading?"

This particular morning, the Holy Spirit directed me—with an audible thought—to continue my reading in the book of Job. I flipped the pages open to the page where I stopped the day before. All l I could do was smile as I read:

> …*the cattle are told of His coming storm.*
>
> JOB 36:33 (AMP)

Whatever it takes, dedicate the time you can to renewing your mind. You'll never regret it. As you read, God quiets the clamoring of the day's demands, establishes your focus on His good plan, and strengthens your spirit with faith.

[4] Head in the Direction of Your Daily Responsibilities & Interests

After we commit our day to God, there's no need for us to stand paralyzed, thinking, *I don't know what to do! I haven't heard anything yet.*

God has preordained the direction for a portion of our days here on Earth by way of the abilities and interests He has given us. When you get up in the morning, head in the direction of the responsibilities your abilities and interests have created.

Divine interruptions

Clearly, part of God's plan for our day is work. A paraphrase of II Thessalonians 3:10 says:

"He who does not work shall not eat."

All of us work inside the home and some of us work both inside and outside. If you're the stay-at-home parent or the last one to leave for work, your day probably begins with the responsibility of feeding someone—even if it's yourself. Certainly in this case there's no need to ask God what to do first. Fix breakfast!

Then, as we get behind the wheel of our daily responsibilities and interests and drive, God's voice will *interrupt* the thoughts directing our behavior at the time.

We should make plans, counting on God to direct us.

PROVERBS 16:9

Many times, when I'm at the grocery store with my mind focused on my list, an audible thought interrupts my train of thinking and directs me to buy an item that isn't on my list. And when I obey, ignoring the reasoning that tells me buying it doesn't make *sense*, I have found myself prepared for surprise dinner guests. Other times I have had the extra item in my pantry to supply someone else's need.

Frequently, the Holy Spirit interrupts my thoughts with, *Stop what you're doing and go home.*

As I have obeyed, I've avoided severe thunderstorms and dangerous ice storms. Other times I have arrived home early to greet unexpected guests. Expect God's voice to interrupt the train of thought that is directing your behavior at the time.

It's important to say that most of the time *God takes the initiative in speaking to us.* We cannot insist that He speak. God took the initiative to speak to Paul on the road to Damascus. God took the initiative to speak with Moses from a burning bush. God took the initiative to speak to the child Samuel.

Then Eli realized it was the Lord who had spoken to the child. So he said to Samuel, "Go and lie down again, and if he calls again, say, 'Yes Lord, I'm listening.'"

I SAMUEL 3:8-9

Although God will usually take the initiative in speaking to us, He does invite us to ask Him for answers.

"Call unto Me and I will answer thee and show thee great and mighty things which thou knowest not."

JEREMIAH 33:3 (KJV)

If any lack wisdom, let Him ask of God...and it will be given to Him.

JAMES 1:5 (KJV)

ASAP Please

There are times when we need an immediate answer from God. Most often those times occur, for me, when I'm in the car.

I live about twenty minutes north of town. And I travel south of town quite often. There are several ways I can go. One route utilizes the highway. The other utilizes side roads. When I come to the main intersection, closest to my house, I have to choose between the two.

Many times when God and I both know I have done my best and yet time is still of the essence, I confidently ask Him, "Lord, should I go straight or turn left and head for the highway?" Instantly I receive clear direction. Best of all, the route He directs me to take opens like the Red Sea. It's wonderful. I bypass traffic jams and encounter far more green lights than red ones.

In Psalm 5, we read of David's plea for immediate direction.

Lord lead me as you promised you would... Tell me clearly what to do, which way to turn.

PSALM 5:8

The King James Version says, "Make your way straight before my face."

I also ask God for immediate direction when I'm lost or turned around. That's still necessary since I have yet to figure out how to work the GPS system on my phone. I don't worry about that. The guidance system I have works perfectly fine.

Again, God's power surrounds His plan. And when we are committed to it, we receive divine direction giving us the time and resources we need to do His plan. In an instant, when God sees that it is necessary, He can communicate to our spirit:

This is the way, walk ye in it.

ISAIAH 30:21 (KJV)

This being said, we must be careful not to treat God as if He were a genie in a bottle. God is not interested in answering questions at our flesh's will just because we want to know the future. God speaks to us in conjunction with His desire for our cooperation in fulfilling His planned purposes. He speaks to give us the wisdom necessary to best fulfill His plans.

We are free to ask God any question. But when some of our questions go unanswered, we need to remember that God has reasons. Many times God withholds direction we long for because circumstances are going to change.

I remember once asking God to help me recall an illustration for a message I was preparing. The day came and went and I never did receive the information I asked for. What I didn't know was that God was going to change the direction of my message. The next morning, He did exactly that and I realized I didn't need the examples I asked for.

More often than not, our unanswered questions are simply barometers to reveal our faith *to us*. A missionary, Helen Roseveare, remembers that she was able to measure her faith in God when He asked her this question, "Will you trust me with this, if I never tell you why?"

At such times, we get to see just how strong our love for God is; how deeply it trusts. Again, God will see to it that we have all the resources we need to do His will during our day. For that adventurous reason, be prepared for God to interrupt your thoughts with His desires as you head in the direction of your daily responsibilities and interests. Rest assured, His direction will come at the exact moment our action is required.

CHAPTER 24

The Grid of Five Questions:

The final to-do necessary in determining whether an audible thought is coming from Mind of Christ or the Mind of the Flesh is this: Run the thought through the grid of five questions. If a persistent thought to take action receives a "yes" answer to one or more of these five questions, it is likely the thought you are hearing is direction from God.

Over the years, I have made hundreds of bookmarks listing these questions. This grid is definitely a great practical help when time is of the essence. Here are the five questions:

Question #1
Does this "audible thought" line up with Scripture?

"...Thy Word is Truth."

JOHN 17:17 (KJV)

Remember, the guidance of God's own Spirit will never lead you in a direction that is contrary to His own written Word. For this reason, the very first question you must ask in determining whether or not a thought that *prompts you to action* is from God must be: Does this thought agree with Scripture?

If you wake up healthy on a Sunday morning and decide you've worked hard enough to earn the right do what you want with your morning, don't expect God's Spirit to endorse staying home if you haven't yet worshipped with other believers. I have had occasion to ask God about skipping church for a variety of reasons. And in answer to my question, He almost always pulls this book from my library of Scripture memory:

> *Not forsaking the assembling of ourselves together, …and so much the more, as ye see the day approaching.*
> HEBREWS 10:25 (KJV)

God's voice will never lead you in a direction that is contrary to Scripture. His written Word is the ultimate source of guidance.

> *Thy Word is a lamp unto my feet and a light unto my path.*
> PSALM 119:105 (KJV)

Again, as II Corinthians 10:5 directs, it's possible to "take captive" or "conquer with a sword," every thought that prompts us to action and make sure it lines up with what the Bible teaches.

Question #2
Does this "audible thought" comply with my God-appointed authorities?

As long as our authorities do not ask us to disobey God's written Word, God's voice will never direct us to disobey them. Hebrews 13:17 (NKJV), speaks of the spiritual authority we are to be under in a church family:

> *Obey those who rule over you, and be submissive, for they watch out for your souls, as those who must give account.*

Romans 13:1 (NKJV), speaks of the authority we are under as employees and citizens:

Let every person be subject to the governing authorities. For there is no authority except from God, and the authorities that exist are appointed by God.

When I exceed the speed limit, I regularly hear: **Obey the laws of the land**, (Romans 13:2).

In that moment, the Holy Spirit is directing me to obey civil authority.

Ephesians 5:22 (ESV) speaks of being under a husband's authority:

Wives, submit to your own husbands, as to the Lord.

Regardless of a husband's motive, if what he asks does not require that you disobey God's Word, comply with the request. God knows exactly what the husband said and why he said it. And He is well able to protect and reward us for our obedience.

At the same time, God gives a husband a wife because of his need for a helpmate. And as helpmates (not nags), God intends that a wife offer alternative suggestions. This is especially true when she believes the information she has might benefit her husband's decision-making process. However, should a husband's original decision stand, every wife can expect God's good purpose to prevail as a result of her submission to her authority's position of leadership. God's voice never directs us to defy those in authority over us.

When I talk about a husband's spiritual authority, this personal example always comes to mind. One afternoon (many years ago now) I was fully prepared for a day of shopping with my three small children. I had successfully managed to dress the four of us and get a grocery list together (which you mothers know can take a day in itself). I was just walking all of us out the door, when my husband called.

Upon asking what I was doing, I quickly explained that I was headed out the door with the children to get some shopping done. He replied by saying he didn't think I should go. Completely frustrated, I controlled my response and politely asked him to tell me why he didn't think I should go. He didn't have a reason. He just didn't think I should. Pitifully, I said, "Okay," and waited some extra seconds hoping he would feel sorry for me and change his mind. He didn't. The conversation came to a close and I hung up the phone.

My attitude was less than desirable. Nonetheless, I took everybody's coats off, laid my keys down, and started thinking about what I could fix for dinner.

I had just reached the kitchen door when the doorbell rang. Not expecting anyone, I opened the door cautiously. There, standing in dirty overalls was a smiling plumber. He explained that he and his crew were ready to pull the new water line I had ordered.

Over time, the water in our purple sink and bathtub faucets had been reduced to a trickle. Now standing with my mouth open, I realized I had completely forgotten about this appointment I had scheduled weeks earlier.

Smiling myself, I cheerfully told him to let me know if he needed anything and headed back to the kitchen to repent over my pitiful attitude. In a matter of days, God's voice, speaking through my authority, treated everyone to a full bathtub of warm water.

Please remember, if you are married, your husband (Christian or not) is not only your authority—he is your priority. He is your most important field of Christian service. God has called you to partner with Him in seeing that your husband is conformed to the image of His Dear Son.

> *For the unbelieving husband is sanctified by the wife, and the unbelieving wife is sanctified by the husband; otherwise your children would be unclean, but now they are holy.*
> I CORINTHIANS 7:14 (KJV)

The sanctification process requires that your husband have confidence in your respect for his direction. As long as our authorities do not ask us to disobey God's Word, God's voice will never direct us to disobey them.

Question #3
Is this "audible thought" directing me to do the opposite of what I feel like doing?

For the desires of the flesh are opposed to the (Holy) Spirit, and the [desires of the] Spirit are opposed to the flesh (Godless human nature); for these are antagonistic to each other...

GALATIANS 5:17 (AMP)

Flesh makes decisions based on feeling. Therefore, if the thought we hear is the *opposite* of what we feel like doing, the majority of the time the direction is coming from the Spirit of God.

When we're in a hurry in a checkout lane and we hear, *Let the person behind you, go in front of you*, it's typically the opposite of what we feel like doing. When we want to go instead of stay and hear, *Don't go now*, that's certainly the opposite of what we feel like doing. When we want to spend money for something we really do need and even have a coupon and yet still hear, *Don't buy it now*, that thought is the opposite of what we feel like doing.

I should say that it's not wrong to want to buy something new with money we have, on a "down day". Neither is it wrong to want to get out of the house when we're bored. These things are only wrong if the Spirit of God directs us not to do them.

A favorite illustration that demonstrates the value of doing the opposite of what we feel like doing has to do with some dishes I wanted to buy years ago. And I need to say these dishes matched my kitchen perfectly. Nonetheless, this lesson began when I picked up an advertisement and saw that my prized dishes were finally on sale.

Feeling sure I was free to purchase them at this advertised, bargain price, I packed up my three small children and headed for the store. Locating the dishes, I joyfully stooped down to pick up the heavy box. And just as I did, I heard, *Don't buy them today.*

I struggled to obey. It was painful. Obeying that directive was definitely the opposite of what I felt like doing. Slowly but surely, however, I stood up, turned my cart around, and left the store. But I should add that—again—I did it with a less than desirable attitude.

Weeks later, I was sitting at my kitchen table, leafing through yet another flyer. As I got about halfway through, I let out a scream. "Hallelujah!" My dishes were now being advertised at an even lower price! Now, it all made *sense!*

Once again, I dressed my children, loaded them in the car, unloaded them from the car, loaded them in a store cart and headed down the store aisle. More eager than ever, I reached, again for my cherished dishes. And to my complete disbelief, I heard, *Don't buy them today.*

By now, I'm sure my children were trying to figure out what kind of shopping Mommy was doing. And they weren't the only ones with questions! Discouraged and frustrated, I mumbled something under my breath, turned my cart around, and gave up on ever bringing the dumb dishes home.

Believe it or not, weeks later, I had actually forgotten about them when a friend called to invite me to investigate a new shopping concept with her called a warehouse club. Quite excited by the thought that there was nothing but bargains at this place, I told her I'd love to go.

Once there, we happily grabbed carts and struck out in different directions. Not wishing to draw out the drama, may I just say, I was stunned when I hit the appliance aisle. There on the bottom shelf was one box of my dishes, at the best price yet. This time, I heard, *Now you can buy them.*

God wanted me to have my new dishes at the very best price. But far more importantly, He wanted me to learn to trust His direction, even when it didn't make sense to me.

When you hear a thought that's the opposite of what you feel like doing, the majority of the time it is direction coming from the Spirit of God. We may not understand God's purpose in asking us to do some of the things He does but I can guarantee you that He has one.

His purpose may be for our benefit; developing our patience while we wait for our time schedule to fit His schedule of blessing. His purpose may be for someone else's benefit. He may be using our behavior to bless another heart that knows Him or to create a desire for Himself in someone that doesn't. When a thought prompts you to action, ask the question, is this thought the opposite of what I feel like doing?" If so, take it from me, you may as well get happy and get after it.

Question #4
Does this audible thought convict me of a particular sin or condemn me?

There is a great difference between feeling *convicted* because we have sinned and feeling *condemned*—generally worthless—for no apparent reason. When we violate scripture, it is the Holy Spirit's job to withdraw, creating conviction in our soul and spirit. He convicts us so we can acknowledge our sin and be free of it.

If a thought convicts us of a specific sin, a particular violation of God's written Word, it is coming from the voice of the Holy Spirit. An example of the Holy Spirit's voice convicting us of a specific sin might sound like, *What you just said was not true— you just lied.*

At that time, it is right to feel and express remorse. The Holy Spirit will direct us to acknowledge our sin before God and make things right with those we have offended. Once we have done so, He will not revisit us with guilt over that mistake.

If, however, we feel condemned or guilty and cannot trace our motives or behavior to a specific sin that we can acknowledge and make right, we know that what we are hearing is the condemning voice of our flesh. Satan and his evil host, through our flesh, will repeatedly work to stop our obedience to God's plan by convincing us that we are not worthy to be used by God.

The mind of the flesh seeks to make us feel condemned two ways. First, the mind of the flesh draws repeated attention to our known failures. Secondly, the mind of the flesh draws our attention to the negative statements or judgments others make about us.

When we allow judgments others make to create feelings of inadequacy or self-hate, we accept condemnation or false guilt. Some examples of those judgmental statements might include:

You don't have time for me.

You can't ever seem to get it right.

You never understand.

You always say the wrong thing.

Notice that the judgments made above are broad generalizations. But, more importantly, such statements do not reflect a specific sin; a law of God that has been broken.

Accepting thoughts of condemnation from our own flesh or from others when our life is free of a specific violation of God's law is allowing our flesh to make us ineffective for the Kingdom of God.

There is therefore now no condemnation to them which are in Christ Jesus, who walk not after the flesh but after the Spirit.

ROMANS 8:1 (KJV)

Jesus' payment with His own blood paid the full price for our sin. Nothing further is required from those of us He died to save. Our acknowledgment of sin before God is all that is needed to restore the full freedom His death provided. We have no reason to accept condemning thoughts that challenge our value to God's kingdom. Convicting thoughts come from the Spirit of God. Condemning thoughts come from satanic forces operating through our flesh.

Question #5
Would the action that came from my thought reflect Jesus?

...all of us, who have had that veil removed, can see and reflect the glory of the Lord. And the Lord—who is the Spirit—makes us more and more like Him as we are changed into his glorious image.

II CORINTHIANS 3:18

Jesus' life was one of servant hood and self-denial. As His disciples, we are in the process of being transformed into His same selfless image. To be sure, this divine transformation is hard on the selfish nature of our flesh. Flesh recoils at the idea of serving others and giving to the needs of others. It far prefers hoarding for itself.

That's why the Mind of our Flesh objects when the Holy Spirit prompts us to give away any of our energies or earthly possessions. We may hear, "They wouldn't do that for you!" or "You will need that someday," or "You have to watch out for yourself. No one else will."

Because Jesus is Himself the humble servant of all, we can be sure the voice of His Spirit will direct us to humbly serve others. An example of one such opportunity that always comes to mind happened when my children were small. I have had few enemies in my lifetime but I did have one neighbor, who was not fond of my children, my dog, or me. At the time this episode took place, I was home-schooling my two oldest children.

Early one morning, the kids and I took a field trip to a fruit farm to pick strawberries. We were very successful. And I had great plans for our berries. I was going to make fresh strawberry pies for my extended family's dessert that evening. Once home, I checked everyone for those unwanted bugs that hang out in berry patches and got started with the business of making pie crust.

Later that afternoon, our German Shepherd, Max, decided to retrieve his rubber ball. It just happened to be resting under my neighbor's side of the fence. As I stepped outside to make a routine check on my children, my neighbor called me over to the fence to let me know she didn't appreciate his efforts.

I apologized sincerely and headed back into the house to finish up the pies and start dinner. I was gazing at my prized pies with great satisfaction, when suddenly I heard, *Take your neighbor one of those pies.*

My stomach dropped. Instantly I felt like I was barreling down a large roller coaster. I said out loud, "Lord, you have got to be kidding me! Oh pleeease!"

There is a verse in scripture that says we shouldn't fear people's faces. But I did fear hers. If ever I struggled to obey God's voice, I did then.

Finally convinced there was no way out, I decided to get it over with. I swallowed hard, hoisted one of the pies into the air, grabbed some whipped cream from the refrigerator, and headed for the fence.

As I got closer, I saw that she was trimming the grass around her flowerbeds with scissors (her yard always did look nice). Realizing I was too close to chicken out, I stammered, "I thought if you hadn't started fixing a dessert for tonight, you and your family might enjoy a strawberry pie."

She looked at the pie and instantly I knew God had picked the right dessert for the occasion.

"If you are friendly only to your friends, how are you different from anyone else?"
MATTHEW 5:47

Soon afterward, we moved closer to the airport to accommodate my husband's busy travel schedule. Years later, I heard through my family that my former neighbor was battling cancer. As they shared the details, I thought back to the day when God asked me to humble myself so that this one He loves could see a reflection of Jesus.

What a priceless opportunity is ours to show the world the Savior. As we have said, all God requires to meet the physical and spiritual needs of His hurting world is our obedience.

Jesus lived and died without the resources of a comfortable home or stocked pantry. Yet He provided for the physical and spiritual needs of the throngs that followed Him by simply following His Father's direction.

"...foxes have holes and birds have nests but the Son of man did not have a place to lay his head."

MATTHEW 8:20 (NIV)

Owning nothing, He provided a seafood lunch for thousands who came to hear Him teach. Owning nothing, he treated His intimate friends to breakfast on the beach. Owning nothing, He even paid taxes with money He was directed to find in the mouth of a fish.

We must never fear that allowing Jesus to live His giving life through us will leave us with less. It is Divine law that in giving, we receive. We cannot out give God. When a thought prompts us to selfless action, we must ask if the action we're being prompted to take reflects Jesus.

Through our behavior, God meets the needs of those who belong to Him. And through our behavior, God reaches to satisfy the spiritual hunger of those who do not. Remember, conflict will always exist as we choose between what seems *reasonable* to our flesh and what is *revealed* to our spirit.

Is God asking you to do something that would reflect the behavior of His dear Son? When what He is asking defies the reason of our human wisdom, we can be sure we're on the right track. Human wisdom is the result of reason. Divine wisdom—how God thinks—is revealed to us from His Written and Spoken Word. God's thoughts and ways are high above ours. Our job is to listen for His direction, trust Him and obey.

CHAPTER 25

The Greatest Benefit of Hearing—Power Over Sin

Without question, my passion for teaching others to hear God's voice has come from my own love for Jesus. And yet as you read these closing chapters, I want to emphasize an important truth: Successfully serving God requires more than the desire to serve Him that passionate love creates. To serve God you and I also need personal freedom; freedom from the power of sin.

In past chapters I have explained how walking in the Spirit gives people like you and me power over the sin that dominates our mortal flesh. Sin can imprison us and actually keep us from doing what we deeply want to do for God. Paul says it best, in this familiar passage:

For I know that nothing good dwells within me, that is in my flesh. I can will what is right, but I cannot perform it. I have the intention and urge to do what is right, but no power to carry it out.

ROMANS 7:18 (AMP)

Although hearing God's voice produces exciting evidence of His existence, my daily interaction with God's Spirit makes it crystal clear that the greatest benefit of being able to hear God's voice is the power over sin it provides. If we want to serve God with the heart of love we have, we must have power over sin.

I've Fallen and I Can't Get Up!

If you are now enslaved or ever have been enslaved to a sinful habit while truly wanting to obey God, you know just how painful the conflict can be. So before we talk more about how hearing God's voice gives us power over sin, let's talk about being entangled in it.

As most of us know, all sin equally separates us from God. One sin separates us no more than another. Yet, if we're honest, there are some sins we don't feel too badly about committing. We typically don't beat ourselves up over slightly exceeding the speed limit, repeating rumors, or watching a questionable television program. We acknowledge the sin rather easily when convicted and, in a flash, we feel free of any guilt.

However, while it is true that all sin separates us equally from God, some sins carry greater consequences than others. For example, drug addictions and eating disorders have particularly serious consequences. And when we struggle with these particular sins, not only do we have trouble getting free from them, we have trouble with the tremendous conflict they cause; the conflict that comes from constant, severe guilt we carry. It certainly shouldn't surprise us that the intensity of our guilt coincides with the intensity of the sin's consequence.

Another such sin is the sin of immorality. The Bible actually tells us the consequences of this sin are some of the worst we can experience. That is true because the sin of immorality is committed against our own body.

*Shun immorality and all sexual looseness—flee from impurity
[in thought, word, or deed]. Any other sin which a man
commits is one outside the body, but he who commits sexual
immorality sins against his own body.*

I CORINTHIANS 6:18 (AMP)

John MacArthur's study notes say it corrupts us at the deepest
human level. It has the power to cripple emotionally and destroy
a body physically. When entangled in this sin, the conflict and
depression that accompanies it can tempt a person to do more
than beat their self up—it can push a person to end their life.

If, as a professing Christian, you have ever been trapped by any
such sins as these, you know how desperate you become to find the
door back to freedom. You become desperate to understand verses
like these two:

*When he died, he died once to break the power of sin. So you
also should consider yourselves to be dead to the power of sin
and alive to God through Christ Jesus.*

ROMANS 6:10 & 11 (NLT)

During my teen years, especially, I remember wondering how
I was ever supposed to succeed at living dead to sin, when even
people like the Apostle Paul said:

*I really want to do what is right but I can't. I do what I don't
want to—what I hate.*

ROMANS 7:15

If that's all Paul had said, you and I might feel free to tolerate
secret sin, knowing we were in good company. But Paul went on
to say:

Thank God! The answer is in Jesus Christ our Lord.

ROMANS 7:25

Uh oh. No pass-go card. Clearly, Paul is telling us there is a way to live free from the power of any sin.

For clarity, it is true that the moment we repent of our sins and commit our life to God's purposes, we receive the free gift of salvation—we get a *new nature* that enables us to desire and obey God. (Romans 6:4) Yet, as we've said, the desire to sin still exists in our unredeemed physical body, rendering us helpless to live without sin under our own power. When we die, we will leave this body behind. But again, until we do, our body's wrong desires fight against the new nature we have.

As much as I wanted to, I couldn't ignore:

For sin shall not have dominion over you…

ROMANS 6:14 (KJV)

Another verse that added to my conflict was this one:

The temptations in your life are no different from what others experience. And God is faithful. He will not allow the temptation to be more than you can stand. When you are tempted, He will show you a way out so that you can endure.

I CORINTHIANS 10:13 (NLT)

Yet, no matter how hard I tried with the discipline *I* could muster, I repeated mistakes. I believed my new nature could free me from bondage to sin, but somehow I kept missing the exit to the way of escape God's Word talked about.

As acknowledged, we will not reach the place—this side of Heaven—where we never sin. But I knew then and have experienced now that it *is possible* to live free from enslaving patterns of sin.

When most people get trapped in sin, they really do try hard to give obedience an honest effort. But, as days of trying go by and they still fail, Christians resign themselves to the reality there's no way out. Consequently they end up living with the mechanical process of telling God they're sorry everyday and acknowledge His forgiveness for whatever sin they've committed.

I tell you earnestly, God's Word is very clear about taking "grace" (the power to do what is right) for granted. It is dangerous to ignore the help God has provided and *tolerate* habitual personal sin (a clear violation of God's commands); counting on God's provision of forgiveness to repeatedly wash it away. Here's what God has to say about a heart that practices sin.

> *If someone claims, "I know God," but doesn't obey God's com-mandments, that person is a liar and is not living in the truth... those who obey God's Word truly show how completely they love Him. That is how we know we are living in Him. Those who say they live in God—should live their lives as Jesus did.*
>
> I JOHN 2:4-6 (NLT)

> *Those who have been born into God's family do not make a practice of sinning, because God's life is in them. So they can't keep on sinning, because they are children of God.*
>
> I JOHN 3:9 (NLT)

I once heard the issue of reoccurring sin in a professing believer's life addressed this way: Proof of a person's salvation is not the absence of sin in daily living. Proof of salvation is found in the determination to keep fighting it.

It's good that we feel grief when we sin. But the more important question is, "Are we legitimately *fighting* to live free of it?"

After a defeating bout of my own, the day came when God helped me see that I was not getting victory over sin for one very simple reason: *I had yet to entrust all of my life to God's complete control.* If that sounds too simplistic, you might need to read it again. The operational word is *complete.*

How patiently God waited for me to submit to the freedom of surrender. How patiently God waits for us all. There were days when God's Presence in a room was so tangible I would run from it to escape Him. In spite of my outright fear of trusting Him, year after year He lovingly pursued my heart.

And, as previously written, when we are determined to run from God, He can use our defiant shortcuts to lead us from the place of fearing Him to the place of trusting Him—in a hurry. Wounded and weary, the day did come when I decided to stop running and wave my tattered flag of surrender. I was desperate to know the healing hiding place that can only be found in Him.

One August day, the Holy Spirit spoke to me about the plans I'd clung to for my own happiness; the ones I'd refused to exchange for His. He said, *All that has been, the destructive ruins left by sin; the wasteland of the dreamlands built by you, has had to be dismantled. Only **my dreams bring refuge** from a world altered and controlled by sin.*

Give Me Three Reasons

Overall, people become entangled in destructive patterns of sin because they don't believe God's plans will bring the satisfaction their plans will. And when someone has believed *that lie*, consciously or unconsciously, they will certainly struggle to be obedient to God. Specifically a Christian who is stuck in patterns of sin has wrongfully believed these 3 things:

[1] A person trapped in sin has believed it's possible to have victory over sin *without* giving complete control of their life to God.

For years I thought that was true. I thought my membership card of salvation entitled me to God's power for my plans when I needed it. I was willing to surrender some of my plans—but not all of them. And for that reason, when it came to particular dreams and interests, I put *distance* between God and myself.

As a result of my choice to willfully edge Him out, I learned the hard way that every area our flesh reserves for itself opens a door for

Satan and sin. Why? Because *our plans have no power to keep Satan away from us or deliver us from sin.* Again, only God's plans contain the power to protect us.

> *So I say, let the Holy Spirit guide your lives. Then you won't be doing what your sinful nature craves.*
>
> GALATIANS 5:16

Any time we reach outside God's purposes to find happiness, we'll be handed a free ticket to Satan's amusement park. May I ask, is there any area of your life you've not yet surrendered to the will of God?

[2] A person trapped in sin has believed their own plans will cause them *less pain* than God's plans will.

To see that this is a definite lie, simply give your own charted plans for pain-free living an honest assessment and see how successful they have been. (I won't be collecting your papers.) Anyone who believes this additional lie will also purposely *distance* himself or herself from God.

Everyone on Earth—Christian or not—inevitably suffers pain as a result of living on a sin-cursed planet. If we're going to suffer one way or another, why wouldn't we want God to use the pain we can't avoid to destroy the power of our flesh and make us like Jesus?

Making the deal better yet, only *God's plans* have the innate ability to transform every problem and pain we suffer into something of *great value*. At any time, He can bring something good out of the brokenness we entrust to Him. Our plans carry no innate power to redeem themselves.

We've got to stop running from pain. When we submit to it, we will find it heightens our sensitivity to God's voice. And that means immediate power.

> *For remember, when your body suffers, sin loses its power...*
>
> I PETER 1:4

It is a spiritual fact that pain presses us in God's direction. If we choose not to panic and instead give God more than a couple of seconds, He will make sure we tangibly get to feel that His grace—His power—is actually sufficient to contentedly sustain us.

As I said in a previous chapter, today I'm living in the very circumstances I hoped most to avoid in life. Yet I repeat: Although I am living in the nest of my greatest fear, I have never been more content. Am I giddy happy always? No—but definitely content.

[3] A person trapped in sin believes power over sin comes from *imitating the behavior of Jesus*—when they choose to.

Many people believe attaining Christ-likeness is like gaining merit badges, similar to the ones some of us worked for in Girl Scouts or Boy Scouts. You try to gain one righteous character at a time by listening to various teachings on the fruits of the Spirit, forgiveness, stewardship and marriage. Once understood, the objective becomes trying hard to imitate what you learned.

Not to burst any bubbles, but human efforts to exhibit godly behavior cannot overcome the sin that controls us. Why? We were not created to develop into sources of our own power. We were created to be containers of God's power by containing God Himself! Listen to these verses:

> *(Jesus) "For it won't be you doing the talking. It will be the Spirit of your heavenly Father speaking through you."*
> MATTHEW 10:20

> *And this is the secret: Christ lives in you.*
> COLOSSIANS 1:27

We cannot overcome sin with sincere effort. Why? Because the Word of God explains that only God can overcome the sin in us by *His own* power.

"Not by might, nor by power, but by my Spirit, says the Lord Almighty—you will succeed because of my Spirit..."

ZECHARIAH 4:6

If you really want freedom from the sin you're in, please read the next few lines over and over until you absorb their deep simple truth. What is your part in the fight for your own freedom? Your part is to wrestle down the alligator of your own will at the time, surrender to Him, and *let Him operate!* That's it!

To be dead to sin, all we have to do is *relinquish our will;* do away with any *distance* we have placed between God and us. Once we do, it is "Spirit Natural" for God's Presence to sweep in and completely possess us—conquering the sin we are powerless to conquer ourselves! That's what this verse is talking about when it says:

I am crucified with Christ: nevertheless I live; yet not I, but Christ liveth in me:

GALATIANS 2:20 (KJV)

On another August day, the Holy Spirit said, *Remember the intent: The Living Christ, my life being captured by mortal flesh, taking on sin in the Earth; walking among the enemy vanquishing its power.*

Mercifully for us all, Jesus has provided a way of escape from the prison of personal sin. And the journey to freedom begins at the same place for all of us—on the threshold of failure. Freedom starts there because failure forces us to understand that we have no power or righteousness to offer God.

One of the sweetest lessons Jesus ever taught me took place as I struggled to look at myself in a shattered looking glass of failure. There, draped in humiliation, I took responsibility for wearing my own crown. And as I did, I heard the loving voice of my Savior invite me to run the fingers of my understanding over His robe of righteousness. In those painful moments, I truly understood for the first time that my value to God had nothing to do with my goodness or strength. I was destitute without His righteousness.

Power over sin begins with our daily choice to live in the state of *surrender*. Once we are dead to sin, Romans 6:11 tells us we ensure victory by living alive unto God. That involves two things: *Staying alert* to God's Presence (Romans 6:11) and *moving in response to His direction*. And we do those two things when we listen for God's voice and do what we hear!

As we have learned, when we walk out the behavior we "hear" we are walking in the Spirit. We walk in the realm of power where no sin can exist. God's voice provides us with the specific escape from every sin we encounter.

Obeying God's direction to postpone shopping until payday, provides an escape from credit card debt. Obeying God's voice of direction to order grilled instead of fried chicken helps provide an escape from the depression of eater's remorse. And finally obeying God's direction to turn down certain dates will provide an escape to the man or woman of His choosing.

Just as a small child's obedience improves when they become aware of their Mother's presence, our obedience improves as we become aware of our Father's Presence. The critical yet simple formula for successfully living dead to sin and alive to God then, is this: SURRENDER, STAY ALERT, AND MOVE! The greatest benefit of hearing God's voice is power over sin.

We can try hard with our own strength and be disillusioned with failure or we can experience power over sin—outside of ourselves—by surrendering our will, staying alert to his Presence and obeying his direction. Nothing can separate us from the sin-conquering power of God's Presence except *our choice to distance ourselves from Him*.

What is the answer then? Stay close to the pacesetter of the ultimate race—the Lord Jesus Christ. Listening to God's voice gives us that opportunity. It's time for us to:

...run with endurance the race that is set before us, looking unto Jesus, the author and finisher of our faith...

HEBREWS 12:1-2 (NKJV)

Are you ready to run the race and win it? Remember the strategy: SURRENDER—STAY ALERT—AND MOVE!

CHAPTER 26

Tell Me What To Expect: S.O.S.

N ow that you're set to run with power and DO what you hear, I thought it might be helpful to let you know what to expect as you begin the adventure of listening for God's voice. Here are three particular areas of your life God's voice will address:

[1] SELF CONTROL—for the Protection of your Physical Body.

As Christians, we have been given the priceless privilege of housing God's Divine Spirit in our own human flesh. And we have learned that we have been given this opportunity so that God can walk out His will on Earth. For this good reason, expect God's voice to address issues of self-control, for the protection of your physical body—His home.

In response to my frequent tendency to push my own physical limits, Mom often reminds me that I only have one body in which to accomplish the will of God. In spite of the fact that I know that's true, it's still always a fight for me to obey the directives I hear about caring for my own physical health.

I believe we ignore thoughts like, *schedule a check-up* and even *put your feet up*, because we think they're our own good ideas. We don't understand they are direction from God. Not to mention, we're busy people. There always seems to be something or someone else that needs to be taken care of first.

A Dastardly Plot

The uncomfortable truth is that many of these so-called distractions that keep us from caring for our health, are purposely orchestrated by our enemy.

> *Be…sober-minded; be vigilant and cautious at all times,*
> *for that enemy of yours, the devil, roams around like a lion*
> *roaring [in fierce hunger], seeking someone to seize upon*
> *and devour.*
>
> I PETER 5:8 (AMP)

Some things are worth considering. And something we should seriously consider is that in the same way God always takes the opportunity to strengthen our lives, Satan always takes the opportunity to destroy them. And, unfortunately for us, Satan's weapon of choice is our own flesh.

We have said that the Mind of our Flesh is a fierce enemy precisely because it lives inside us and is bent on destroying itself. That may sound harsh, but we all know that if we allowed our flesh to satisfy every desire it has, our body and mind would both be destroyed.

> *…following after the old nature leads to death.*
>
> ROMANS 8:6

Again, if you doubt that's true, open the menu at any restaurant and ask yourself what looks good. Or simply pay attention to the particular reading material your eyes are drawn to in a grocery store checkout lane. Paul said:

...who will release and deliver me from (the shackles of) this body of death?

ROMANS 7:24 (AMP)

Get With the Program

Our flesh has the power to destroy itself because it has no internal mechanism of self-control. If you've tried to diet lately, you know that's true. Although it is possible to temporarily discipline our flesh, in and of itself, it cannot regulate its desires. Why? Galatians 5:23 answers the question. The verse states that self-control is a fruit (a characteristic) of God's Spirit. In other words, self-control comes from God. To experience self-control, then, the Spirit of God must be in control of us.

For this reason, we can expect God's voice to call us to self-control. I know that whenever I hear, *Turn off the television and go to sleep*, I'm hearing God's voice. I know it's God's voice because my flesh would much rather channel surf through mindless nonsense all hours of the night.

Once I take notice of what God wants me to do, the choice is mine. I can obey what I hear and step into the power of self-control that surrounds God's plan for me—and receive the benefit—or not. In this case, there is a specific benefit of sleeping between the hours of 10:00 pm and 2:00 am—the time I'm tempted to stay up. It is cellular renewal. Interestingly, cellular renewal takes place as a result of strategic healing hormones that are produced in the body only at that time. Again:

Following after the Holy Spirit leads to life and peace...

ROMANS 8:6

Whenever I hear, *Eat at home tonight*, I know that direction is coming from God. Primarily because my flesh likes to do the opposite—eat out! But more conclusively, statistics clearly indicate it's the additives and fat in the fast food we are eating that cause serious health problems in America.

Whenever I hear, *Drink water*, I know for sure I'm hearing God's voice. At any time, my flesh would rather have pop, (coke or a soft drink—depending on where you live).

If we believe what we hear is the result of our own knowledge we'll tend to dismiss the direction or put it off for later. And that can be dangerous—especially if what we've been prompted to do has serious implications for others we love or ourselves.

The power of our own good intentions breaks down easily. We may never get around to doing what we were told to do. Many times, I reach the end of the day and realize that, although I intended to, I didn't drink any water at all!

You have read the benefits of hearing God's voice are tied to immediate obedience. When God gives us a directive, He intends that we obey immediately. If we wait, we may miss the blessing of His direction. My mom has always reminded me that obedience that is not immediate—is not obedience.

In light of that truth, a good way to determine whether or not a thought is from God is to listen for your flesh to begin making *excuses*. When you hear yourself making excuses for not doing what you just heard, you can bet your flesh is working to cheat you out of the benefit of the Holy Spirit's direction. Have you ever heard this with your inside ears? *Go back in the house and grab an umbrella.* If so I'd be willing to bet you've also spent some soggy moments wishing you had.

When you hear, *Get dressed* or, *Comb your hair*, it's important to obey. God alone may know there's unexpected company headed in your direction. Inside and outside, our bodies are the home of the living God. The King of Heaven has chosen to robe Himself in our humanity. Our representation of Him should be nothing less than our best.

The sinful nature of our flesh always makes it easy to abuse our temple. But if we do, we risk losing the health and strength God has given us to do His will. Because God lives in you, in the days ahead, expect God's voice to address areas of self-control for the protection of your physical body.

[2] ORDER—For Efficiency in Doing God's Will

All of God's children are born with a "to do" list for His Kingdom. And with every passing day, the ongoing fulfillment of Biblical prophecy that is broadcast on our nightly news makes it clear that time is running out on the clock of human history. Jesus' return is very soon. Yet the one human commodity we do need, to accomplish God's will, is time. Jesus Himself said:

> *"We must quickly carry out the tasks assigned us by the one who sent us. The night is coming, and then no one can work."*
>
> JOHN 9:4 (NLT)

While we're talking about work, if your home repair projects have been anything like mine, you may be able to identify with the frustration that accompanies searching for missing tools.

I can remember a time when I gave up searching for some missing wallpaper tools; deciding it would be quicker to go to the store and buy new ones. I changed my grubby work clothes and grabbed my purse only to find that my keys were missing too. By the time I found the keys, bought what I needed, got back from the store and started the job—the day was half over. What's my point? Order facilitates efficiency. We need look no further than to the order displayed in nature to know that God is a God of order.

> *All things should be done with regard to decency and propriety and in an orderly fashion.*
>
> I CORINTHIANS 14:40 (AMP)

Because God wants us to accomplish the work of His will before He returns for us, expect God to speak to bring order to your life. How will He do that? By giving direction regarding your daily responsibilities. They comprise most of your day. Therefore, they are the raw material God uses to build discipline and character in us. And the wonderful result of discipline and character is order in our lives and in our homes.

Cranking it Out!

Today, the level of productivity I experience for God's kingdom continues to surprise even me. I know it's all the result of God's grace. But, practically speaking, I can contribute the increase of effectiveness to the order that God continues to establish in my life and home. This order is being solely produced by my obedience to God's direction throughout the course of my daily responsibilities.

On any given day, God's direction may be as simple as, *Stop what you're doing and be on time.*

If I step over shoes I've kicked off earlier, I will hear, *Go back and pick them up.*

If I'm on the phone too long, I will hear, *Hang up.*

And when I'm in bed too long, I will hear, *Get up!*

You, too, can be fairly sure that when you hear any one of those three "ups"—pick up, hang up or get up, the direction is coming from God.

The audible thought, *Do the dishes*, is not generally one generated by my flesh. I have no trouble clearing the dishes off the table but I do have a tendency to let them sit in the sink! There are reasons for God's promptings. A lack of order in our homes wastes time and wasted time certainly makes us less productive. Again, as I continue to do what God tells me to do, when He tells me to do it, I am delightfully surprised to find that everything on both our lists keeps getting done.

First Things First

God will not only use these everyday responsibilities to build character and discipline in us, He will also use them to point out weaknesses that exist in our character. Procrastination was a weakness He needed to point out in mine.

Back when my husband traveled extensively, the responsibility for home and farm repairs fell to me. With all the hats I wore as a home-schooling Mom, when a particular repair wasn't an emergency, I put it off.

Over time, as I listened for God's instruction each morning, I began to see a pattern develop. I noticed that He almost always directed me to tackle first the responsibility I dreaded most.

One particular day, as I took out the trash, I noticed our aging hot tub had sprung a small leak. Fully planning to deal with the problem later, I turned to go back into the house. And as I did, I immediately heard, *Schedule a service call.*

The voice was so insistent that I couldn't ignore it, (although I tried). The only service company I could think of was an hour from our home. I reasoned that a secretary would wait for other business in the area before sending anyone my way—so I saw no reason to rush to the phone. Nonetheless, the persistent, insistent voice prodded me to pick up the phone and call. I did. Expecting an answering machine, I actually stuttered when a pleasant voice that belonged to the owner picked up the phone. I said, "Hello, this is Mrs. Carroll and I have a hot tub with a leak."

He said, "Mrs. Carroll you just caught me. Typically, I'm not in the office today but I was just walking through the warehouse to get some paperwork and I heard the phone ringing. I'll be in your area tomorrow so I'll stop by and see if I can help you out."

The next day, he made the hour trip and fixed my leak. God is eager to help us accomplish our work so we can be available for His. I'm happy to say, to this good day, I have learned to tackle the worst—first. Expect God to use your daily responsibilities to reveal and rebuild your character weaknesses as He calls you to a life of self-control and order.

[3] SACRIFICE—The Fear Factor

There is a wholesome fear that God has given us to protect our life. But there is also a "spirit of fear," that II Timothy 1:7 tells us is not from God. And it happens to be the weapon our flesh will use when it wants to stop us from taking sacrificial steps of obedient faith.

I taught my Sunday school children, age's three to six, about the Armor of God listed in Ephesians chapter 6. In an effort to help them understand that Satan cannot be resisted with physical strength, I created the following rhyme: It will not help for me to say, 'Satan, please, go away!' No—I must speak like God's Son. Say, 'It is written!'—and watch him run!

Regardless of our age or size, it's right and necessary that you and I talk back to a spirit of fear with a verse from the Word of God. And fear can raise its ugly head when we least expect it. A spirit of fear can flare anytime we are asked to give up anything that provides us with a sense of security; the comfort of possessions, money, family and friends or the intangible things we value, like acceptance by others.

A spirit of fear insists that *it's clinging to what we have* that will keep us safe and make us happy. But that's not true. The opposite is true.

> *"For whoever is bent on saving his [temporal] life [his comfort and security here], shall lose [eternal life]; and whoever loses his life [his comfort and security here] for My sake shall find [life everlasting]."*
>
> MATTHEW 16:25 (AMP)

We know, from the life of Jesus, that it's a life of sacrifice that brings satisfaction and reward. Jesus offered up His life in order that we be spared from Hell eternally and enjoy reconciliation to God for eternity. He was rewarded for His sacrifice.

Therefore, God elevated Him to the place of highest honor and gave him the name above all other names, that at the name of Jesus every knee should bow, in heaven and on earth and under the earth…

PHILIPPIANS 2:9-10 (NLT)

As long as the direction we hear lines up with Scripture, we must never let a spirit of fear stop us from sacrifice for Jesus' sake. Flesh delights in using fear as a curtain to hide God's blessing. For that reason, when fear is the reason why my flesh hesitates to obey God, I take it as a green light to run forward. For not only does God send lavish grace to keep us standing through fear of pain and sacrifice, He rewards us in this life and in the next for the rich redemption it brings to others.

But thanks be to God, Who in Christ always leads us in triumph…and through us spreads and makes evident the fragrance of the knowledge of God everywhere,

II CORINTHIANS 2:14 (AMP)

There's nothing like the sweet fragrance of flowers and freshly mown grass after a spring shower. To break sin's power and bring the refreshing perfume of redemption to those around you, expect God's voice to call you to face your fear of sacrifice.

A Lifelong Enemy

Now that I'm a grandmother, you'd think my spiritual enemies (like that of fear) would be losing some of their strength—like the rest of my body! Yet, my spiritual enemies remain strong as ever. Even after years of God's faithful provision, I never hear, *Pay your tithe*, without having to resist my flesh's fear of running short. Additionally, I never hear God say, *Give that away*, without having to resist the fear that I'll go without. It's pitifully sad—but oh, so true.

Our flesh's thinking is upside down compared to the wisdom of God. His ways cannot be reasoned out.

A Palette of Problems

Fear has no boundaries. Not only can it plague us with anxiety over the loss of material possessions, like a cancer, it can spread to destroy every blessing God has given us—including the blessing of relationships. If we're not careful, fear keeps us from reaching out to be enriched by others and even uses us to hold others back from the richness of God-ordained opportunities. Perhaps the greatest challenge we face in this world is learning how to hold the things we love loosely.

Several years ago, God's voice called me to face my fear of releasing the people I love to His plan. I handled my children leaving home for college relatively well. I even helped my oldest son Charlie and his wife Amy move to South Carolina, where they spent the first five years of their marriage. In spite of those particular successes, over the years God has continued to see that my faith receives a good stretching now and then.

One morning, as I watched a TV commercial about a Hillsong Conference in Australia, I sat straight up in bed. I did it when I clearly heard God say—through an audible thought—*I want your son Micah, to go to that conference.*

Instantly, I became fearful. As ridiculous as it sounds, I actually wondered if it would help for me to sit really still. Maybe God wouldn't say it again. But He did say it again, and when He did, I said out loud, "God, you actually want me to put my son on a plane—by himself—and send him across the ocean to Australia?" In His quiet way, God let me know I had heard Him correctly the first time. For several days my fearful flesh consoled itself with the thought that my son wouldn't be interested.

Two weeks later, when Micah came home for Spring Break, I brought the subject up quite casually. "By the way, Micah, is there any chance you would be interested in going to the Hillsong Conference in Australia this summer?"

I don't think I finished the sentence before he raised his voice. "Are you kidding? I've been listening to their newest album all week. I would love to go!"

Smiling on the outside, the only thought I had on the inside was, *Oh great, now what do I do?*

That happens to be a question God loves to answer. In seconds, God ran me through the paces of His truth, reminding me that no one is ever safer anywhere than they are when they are in the center of His plan. There was no arguing with that. So I thanked God for His patience with me. And every time a spirit of fear approached, I used it as a signal to thank God for the blessing He had for Micah in Australia.

God confirmed His plan by sending funds, outside of my budget, to pay for the trip. And when Micah came back, he said, "That trip set the course for my whole life."

Facing a Real Giant

I have dealt with a lot of pain in my day, but in some respects even childbirth seems like a walk in the park compared to the pain of being rejected by someone you love. The fear of rejection is one of the primary reasons people resist obeying God's voice. The concept of surrendering to God's direction suggests we give up our right to be protected from such pain. And who wants to purposefully subject themselves to rejection?

Family relationships were created by God to bring us great pleasure. The very Body of Christ is built from the living cells of families. We shouldn't be surprised, then, that Satan delights in using them for target practice.

Someone has recently described the *break up* of a home as nothing less than the murder—the beheading—of a family. What suffering and dysfunction children of all ages are enduring at this moment. Satan and his demons are consumed with their destructive pastime; that of annihilating families and splintering relationships.

In the face of this darkness, we should not be surprised that restoration is God's favorite business. However, for God's healing and reconciliation to take place in our homes and relationships, we have to acknowledge that someone has to put Jesus on and take the first step. This being true, God's voice directs us to confront our fear of being vulnerable to rejection.

The thought of approaching particular people might make you and I swallow hard. But either our lives are surrendered to the Holy Spirit's use or they are not. I have often heard that God's will—will never lead us where His grace won't keep us. If God desires to restore a relationship, through you, His grace will sufficiently hold you through your fear of being rejected in the process. To disobey the prompting of God because we fear rejection is to deny Jesus the opportunity to restore an eternal soul and the lives that surround it.

Anytime fear of rejection is the reason you and I won't say something as simple as, "I love you," or "I forgive you," we can be sure forces of darkness are working to stop the redeeming power of God from bringing radical change to a hurting heart—even if the heart is our own.

If you are currently estranged from a family member or friend and hear the thought, *Call them and tell them you were thinking about them*, you can be sure the voice you hear is coming from the heart of your Redeemer, Jesus Christ.

Never forget that being a powerful Christian is not about how much courage you can muster up to do God's will. It's about *surrendering your will*. It's about receiving a front row seat to watch the sin-shattering power of God do its own work through you. God's voice calls us to face our fear of being vulnerable. What relationship does God want to restore through you?

Additionally, God's voice calls us to face our fear of standing for truth. And that usually means He calls us to stand apart from popular opinion. When you and I can clearly identify God's voice, we can easily stand alone. In a very lonely place of standing alone, Job resolutely said:

"...though He slay me, yet will I serve Him."

JOB 13:15 (NKJV)

It is mind-boggling but true that while people admire those who stand alone, they often question the need for the very stand the people take. I believe that's because it's easier for them to question the stand than face their own fear of being asked to do the same thing.

Our purposes are all different. God does not ask some of us to do what He asks others to do. He gives us all different grace because His purposes for us are different.

If God's purposes for you call you to take drastic steps of obedience, don't be surprised if family and friends question the stand you take. It's to be expected. It's hard for all of us to watch those we love struggle or suffer. Nonetheless, with the praise of men or without it, following God's direction yields amazing grace to ensure that you accomplish His revealed will.

Christ is our example. He lived and died enduring the scorn of popular opinion in order that you and I might know the freedom of redemption. And He received the strength He needed to obey because God's power and strength surrounded His plan for His Son.

In my own life I have seen that radical redemption in the lives of those we love sometimes requires that we endure radical suffering.

...if we are to share His glory, we must also share His suffering.

ROMANS 8:17 (NLT)

If God's plan for you allows radical suffering at the enemy's hand, you can be certain God's outcome includes a radical reward of redemption. Expect God's voice to call you to sacrifice.

CHAPTER 27

Final Thoughts

The Confirmation of Peace

When my son Charlie was young, his favorite possessions on Earth were his G.I. Joe soldiers. And he had quite the collection, until they ended up as targets for bee-bee gun practice. I believe he's forgiven his younger brother for that. At any rate, the soldiers were marketed with this slogan: Now you know. And knowing is half the battle.

Hopefully you now know what to expect regarding Satan's use of fear to thwart your obedience to God. Please remember that, up until the moment you *do* what God has asked, your fearful flesh will passionately beg you listen to *reason* and abort your righteous intentions. Yet the instant you do obey, God will confirm that you've done the right thing by flooding your heart with *a sense of His peace.*

Peace is the confirmation of God's will. It's the inner calm that dissolves fear. It is a quietness, sent by God, to the center of our being that assures you your circumstances are safely in Divine control in spite of what your natural eyes see.

The inner call to obey God may create a sense of anxiety for a moment. But that anxiety melts into peace the instant we submit.

Whenever your personal sense of peace is disturbed in the course of daily living, never hesitate to abort the mission—abandon your activity until time in God's Presence redirects your steps.

Thou wilt keep him in perfect peace whose mind is stayed on Thee because he trusteth in Thee.

ISAIAH 26:3 (KJV)

But the mind of the (Holy) Spirit is life and soul-peace [both now and forever].

ROMANS 8:6B (AMP)

A Sure-Fire Test

We are never more desperate for God's direction than we are during a time of crisis. Yet that seems to be one of the most difficult times to discern His Voice.

To offset the confusion strong emotions can create in crisis, it's imperative that we take whatever time is necessary to regain a sense of peace before we listen for what God is saying to our spirit. Although we would like to believe our first thoughts are from God, that's rarely the case when strong emotion is involved.

In such cases it's also important to say we should never hesitate to tap into the godly counsel the Body of Christ provides. Many times, the counsel I have received has clarified God's direction; even though the direction God clarified, at times, differed from the counsel I received. Maybe you can remember asking a friend to help you choose between two items in a store. Their opinion either confirmed your original choice or made you sure you wanted the item they didn't care for.

Personally, to be sure I'm hearing God's voice correctly when emotion runs high, I always ask myself, "Am I willing to let some time pass before I act—to confirm that what I am hearing is from God?"

If I believe God has prompted my course of action, I will be willing to wait for confirmation.

Don't be impatient, wait for the Lord.

PSALM 25:14

If an anxious voice prods me to take action to the extent that I am fearful and therefore unwilling to wait, I can be sure the voice speaking is that of my flesh's fear, anger or wounded pride. Even the mind of the flesh knows "haste makes waste." Therefore, it speaks loudly—hoping to push me to premature action.

In contrast, there will be no clamoring push from the voice of God's Spirit. He has all the time and power necessary to handle every problem. All God needs is our obedience to His direction to bring calm out of chaos.

Reasons We Miss God's Direction

I would like to be able to tell you that for all my studying and life experience, I always get it right—always hear accurately what God is saying and respond accordingly. But I don't. For now, my feet are still made of clay. Yet even my failures are valuable. Why? Each one motivates me to listen more closely.

I have pinpointed three major reasons I miss hearing what God is saying. First, I fail to hear what God is saying when busy times cause me to neglect time in His Written Word. Secondly, I do miss God's direction when I let my emotions take the lead. And finally, I miss hearing God's voice of direction when I'm too committed to my own plans to be open to His.

On the days you're sure you heard God's voice and the evidence indicates that you did not, don't allow Satan to use the experience to affect your faith. Trust will call you to try again. And as you do, always be encouraged that you are making it your purpose to know God's mind and obey His will.

The Adversary's Defiance

Many years ago I wrote these words on a paper plate and taped it to my refrigerator. "Proof of God's Presence is the Adversary's Defiance." Eventually I cut away the rim of the plate and kept only the important part. That circle of paper hangs there today. The converse has been expressed, "If the Devil is leaving us alone, it is because we present no threat to his kingdom."

The more intimate and therefore powerful our relationship with God becomes, the more fire we draw from the enemy. Satan's power is no match for the power of God. Yet he is a fearsome combatant for unarmed flesh.

As we face the reality of this warfare, we must always be prepared to do first what Jesus did when He was attacked by Satan—strike back by quoting God's Written Word. Next, we must seek the refuge the direction of His Voice provides.

The more ground you and I take for God's glorious Kingdom as a result of doing His will, the more vital the comfort and strength of His voice becomes. Recently, as I worked to write a portion of the material you are reading, the enemy's opposition became tangible. Without warning, groundless thoughts of failure over completing the work overwhelmed me. Audible thoughts that were not mine, full hopelessness and despair, attacked the sense of peace I had enjoyed moments before. Without waiting for me to formulate a prayer, God's voice directed me to get up from my desk and walk outside. Feeling anxious and weak I climbed the stairs, opened the door, and walked out to the steps that lead down to the open meadow of our backyard.

The Comforter's Reliance

As soon as I reached the steps, a soft gust of wind embraced me. And there, on the top step, in a still moment of warm sunshine I heard God say, *Marty, it's not by your might nor by your power, but by my Spirit.*

God's voice alone silences the voice of the enemy when it attacks the truth of God.

> *...when the enemy shall come in like a flood, the Spirit of the LORD shall lift up a standard against him.*
>
> ISAIAH 59:19 (KJV)

Instantly, the tormenting spirits that oppressed me fled and I was physically drenched in a shower of soul-saturating peace. Strengthened inside and out, I hurried back inside to finish my writing. For wonderful reasons like this one, the Holy Spirit is called the Comforter. Speaking of the Holy Spirit:

> *"But the Comforter (Counselor, Helper, Intercessor, Advocate, Strengthener, Standby), the Holy Spirit, Whom the Father will send in My name [in My place, to represent Me and act on My behalf], He will teach you all things. And He will cause you to recall—will remind you of, bring to your remembrance—everything I have told you."*
>
> JOHN 14:26 (AMP)

When It's All Been Said and Done

The purpose of this book has been to equip you with the knowledge you need to discern God's sweet voice of direction in your daily living. As your conversations increase, you will fall ever more passionately in love with God. As a result, fierce courage will overtake your fears; enabling you to fulfill the desires of His heart. I can only smile as I imagine the divine results of your obedience to His dear voice.

> *"I will instruct you and teach you in the way you should go; I will counsel you with My eye upon you."*
>
> PSALM 32:8 (AMP)

Will you allow God to renew your mind? Will you begin saturating your mind with the Word and commit Scripture to memory so that the Holy Spirit can speak clearly to your spirit?

Audible thoughts from the mind of your flesh will always challenge God's voice but they can be outnumbered as you build a library of the knowledge of God within your spirit. From your library, God's Spirit will bring truth to mind and give you direction. Jentezen Franklin has said, "When you can't hear God, read God. And when you read God you'll hear God."[12]

God may speak to you with the truth of Scripture you already know or in an instant He can speak to you with immediate revelation for the situation you face. However He chooses to speak, rest assured there is no reason to fear God's direction. His grace will always flow lavishly to anyone who dares to stand through any pain that obedience may bring.

This is an exciting time in history to be enlisted as a Soldier of Light. The foundation of our nation is shaking. But God in us can restore America's stability through us as we are held steady by God's own hand. II Chronicles 15:15 is a picture of my prayer for this great nation:

> *All were happy for this covenant with God, for they had entered into it with all their hearts and wills, and wanted him above everything else, and they found him! And he gave them peace throughout the nation.*

I challenge you to begin listening for God's voice in the audible thoughts that come from His spirit. As you identify His voice prompting you to action take the time to record the direction in a journal. The record of His guidance and the results that follow will bolster your faith in God's good purposes and encourage you on. Practice makes progress. Remember the battle plan: *Surrender, stay alert and move!*

The adventure of discerning and obeying God's voice is a privilege to which I am hopefully addicted. A personal paraphrase of I John 1:3 says it best:

I have told you about what I myself have actually experienced so that you may have the fellowship and joys of intimate conversation I have with the Father and with Jesus Christ his Son!

May God grant us all abundant grace in these last days to be marvelously transformed into the Holy image of Jesus. And may our love burn a blazing trail of light for the lost as we listen and follow after the Sound of His Voice!

ACKNOWLEDGEMENTS

I'd like to thank:

My sisters for their many prayers on behalf of the book and each *Jesus First* friend who prayed for this project!

A dear friend and Pastor for your editing contributions to the foundational chapter of this book. Your knowledge of God's Word and love for His Kingdom kept my doctrinal compass due North! To God be the Glory!

Faithful friends, Rachel, Greg, and Carolyn, for your willingness to give the manuscript a first read. I appreciate each constructive comment you made and further appreciate the inspiration of your steady pace, in the great race of faith. My run is richer for your friendship.

Jan and Bob Hartenstein and Innkeeper Ministries in Lewisburg, Ohio for the haven of Sabbath rest you provided for my writing. Your love for laborers is making an eternal difference. The atmosphere of God's Presence and peace brings Heaven to Earth. May God continue to richly bless all who give their time and resources to the work of Innkeeper Ministries. And may He hasten the fulfillment of His purposes in every servant who finds welcome *room in your Inn.*

Lisa Von De Linde of LisaVDesigns, my kind cohort in completing the work. God used your artful skill, experience, and knowledge of "the ropes," to pull me to the finish of a life long climb! Thank you for ALL your hard work. I am forever grateful.

Endnotes

1. *The Daily Walk Bible.* Wheaton: Tyndale House Publishers, Inc., 1987. Print.

2. "Poll: Most Americans Say They're Christian," ABCNEWS/Beliefnet poll, accessed June 24, 2006, http://abcnews.go.com/US/story?id=90356&page=1&singlePage=true

3. Sampson, Marty and Zsech, Darlene. "One Thing." *Savior King.* Hillsong Music Australia, 2007. CD.

4. MacArthur, John. *The MacArthur Study Bible (New King James Version).* Nashville: Thomas Nelson, Inc, 1997. Print.

5. Hallett, John. "There's No Disappointment In Jesus." 1940.

6. Colbert, M.D., Don. *The Bible Cure for Memory Loss.* Lake Mary: Siloam Press, 2001. Print.

7. "Three in Four Americans Believe in Paranormal," GALLUP poll, accessed June 16, 2005, http://www.gallup.com/poll/16915/three-four-americans-believe-paranormal.aspx

8. Suffield, Kitty. "Little Is Much When God Is In It." 1924. Public Domain.

9. Stern, Richard. *The Hole In Our Gospel.* Nashville: W Publishing an imprint of Thomas Nelson, 2009, 2010, 2014. Print.

10. "Editorial: Campus in need of sex talk," Baylor Lariat Archives, Survey conducted in 2006 by Byron Weathersbee, accessed September 19, 2007, http:// www.baylor.edu/lariatarchives/news.php?action=story&story=46943

11. Colbert, M.D., Don. *The Bible Cure for Memory Loss.* Lake Mary: Siloam Press, 2001. Print.

12. Franklin, Jentezen. *Kingdom Connection* (Santa Ana, CA: TBN - Trinity Broadcasting Network).

Made in the USA
San Bernardino, CA
07 December 2015